W9-AGF-672

From The New Zealand Prayer Book:

*O, thou most holy and beloved, my companion, my
Guide upon the way, my bright evening star.*

By Madeleine L'Engle

★ BRIGHT EVENING STAR ★

MYSTERY OF THE INCARNATION

MADELEINE L'ENGLE

HAROLD SHAW PUBLISHERS
WHEATON, ILLINOIS

© 1997 by Crosswicks, Inc.

All rights reserved. No part of this book may be reproduced or transmitted in any form or by any means, electronic or mechanical, including photocopying, recording, or any information storage and retrieval system without written permission from Harold Shaw Publishers, Box 567, Wheaton, Illinois 60189. Printed in the United States of America.

ISBN 0-87788-079-4

Cover design by David LaPlaca

Library of Congress Cataloging-in-Publication Data

L'Engle, Madeleine.
    Bright evening star : mystery of the Incarnation / Madeleine L'Engle.
        p. cm.
    ISBN 0-87788-079-4
    1. Jesus Christ—Biography. 2. Incarnation—Meditations. 3. L'Engle, Madeleine. 4. Christian biography. I. Title.
    BT301.2.L36 1997
    232'.1—dc21   97-21410
                                                                      CIP

02 01 00 99 98 97

10 9 8 7 6 5 4 3 2 1

To Colin and Maura, Nancy and Albert,
Kay and Jimmy, Charlene and Bobby,
Sally, and Joan, and all who have
been christs for me.

CONTENTS

A SKY FULL OF CHILDREN

CHAPTER 1

I WALK OUT ONTO THE DECK OF MY COTTAGE, looking up at the great river of the Milky Way flowing across the sky. A sliver of a moon hangs in the southwest, with the evening star gently in the curve.

Evening. Evening of this day. Evening of the century. Evening of my own life.

I look at the stars and wonder. How old is the universe? All kinds of estimates have been made and, as far as we can tell, not one is accurate. All we know is that once upon a time or, rather, once before time, Christ called everything into being in a great breath of creativity—waters, land, green growing things, birds and beasts, and finally human creatures—the beginning, the genesis, not in ordinary Earth days; the Bible makes it quite clear that God's time is different from our time. A thousand years for us is no more than the blink of an eye to God. But in God's good time the universe came into being, opening up from a tiny flower of nothingness to great clouds of hydrogen gas to swirling galaxies. In God's good time came solar systems and planets and ultimately this planet on which I stand on this autumn evening as the Earth makes its graceful dance around the sun. It takes one Earth day, one Earth night, to make a full turn, part of the intricate pattern of the universe. And God called it good, very good.

A sky full of God's children! Each galaxy, each star, each living creature, every particle and sub-atomic particle of creation, we are all children of the Maker. From a sub-atomic particle with a life span of a few seconds, to a galaxy with a life span of billions of years, to us human creatures somewhere in the middle in size and age, we are made in God's image, male and female, and we are, as Christ promised us, God's children by adoption and grace.

Children of God, made in God's image. How? Genesis gives no explanations, but we do know instinctively that it is not a physical image. God's explanation is to send Jesus, the incarnate One, God enfleshed. Don't try to explain the Incarnation to me! It is further from being explainable than the furthest star in the furthest galaxy. It is love, God's limitless love enfleshing that love into the form of a human being, Jesus, the Christ, fully human and fully divine.

Christ, the Second Person of the Trinity, Christ, the Maker of the universe or perhaps many universes, willingly and lovingly leaving all that power and coming to this poor, sin-filled planet to live with us for a few years to show us what we ought to be and could be. Christ came to us as Jesus of Nazareth, wholly human and wholly divine, to show us what it means to be made in God's image. Jesus, as Paul reminds us, was the firstborn of many brethren.

I stand on the deck of my cottage, looking at a sky full of God's children, knowing that I am one of many brethren, and sistren, too, and that Jesus loves me, this I know, for the Bible tells me so.

Bathed in this love, I go into the cottage and to bed.

Small, beloved child.

I am probably less than two years old, sitting in my grandmother's lap. We are on the porch at the beach house. Her old green rocking chair creaks back and forth as she rocks me. A white coquina ramp runs east from the porch steps, across the green and prickly scrub, onto the beach. At the foot of the ramp the sand is soft and deep, for the tides do not reach this high and it gets wet only when it rains. Near the ocean the sand is firm and patterned by the wavelets which flow and ebb with the tides. Above the water the stars are brilliant. The high dunes on which the cottage stands are part of a wide, still wild world, but I feel safe, held in my grandmother's strong arms. She has a high, sweet voice, and she winds the deeper safety of her words into the soft night air as she sings and rocks, sings and rocks.

> *Jesus, tender shepherd, hear me.*
> *Bless thy little lamb tonight.*
> *Through the darkness be thou near me.*
> *Keep me safe till morning light.*

Jesus, the Christ, Maker of the Universe. Thank you, Jesus, for being born for me. For being part of my life, always.

Was there a moment, known only to God, when all the stars held their breath, when the galaxies paused in their dance for a fraction of a second, and the Word, who had called it all into being, went with all his love into the womb of a young girl, and the universe started to breathe again, and the ancient harmonies resumed their song, and the angels clapped their hands for joy?

Power. Greater power than we can imagine, abandoned, as the Word knew the powerlessness of the unborn child, still unformed, taking up almost no space in the great ocean of amniotic fluid, unseeing, unhearing, unknowing. Slowly growing, as any human embryo grows, arms and legs and a head, eyes, mouth, nose, slowly swimming into life until the ocean in the womb is no longer large enough, and it is time for birth.

My awareness of this momentous event of the birth of Jesus was known to me only in metaphor when I was a child.

I grew up in New York, the only child of older parents, most of whose friends worked in the world of the arts, who were singers, dancers, actors. At Christmastime my parents held open house on Sunday evenings, and a dozen or more people gathered around the piano, and the apartment was full of music, and theology was sung into my heart.

Joy to the world! the Lord is come . . .

While shepherds watched their flocks by night . . .
And glory shone around. . . .

Away in a manger, no crib for a bed.
The little Lord Jesus lay down his sweet head. . . .

Let nothing you dismay . . .
O tidings of comfort and joy . . .

O come, let us adore Him. . . .

> *Hark! the herald angels sing,*
> *"Glory to the newborn King!"*

Thank you, thank you!

My prayers at night started with thanks, thanks to Jesus for being part of our lives. Prayers of sorrow for anything I had done wrong during the day. Prayers of comfort and immediate forgiveness.

My parents taught me a God of love, yet a demanding God who expected me to be honorable and truthful but who also allowed me to ask questions.

Why was there war? My birth had come shortly after the end of what used to be called the Great War, and all my life I had heard people talking about the war and power; it was the most righteous and powerful nations who won the terrible war. But why was there war at all?

Why were my father's lungs burned with mustard gas?

Are the Germans bad? Why do we call them Huns?

Do they believe in Jesus, too?

Does God love them?

Yes. God loves. God is love.

God loves us even when we do wrong, but God does not love the wrong we do.

My parents tried to answer me honestly and reasonably. We went to church together on Sunday. I did not go to Sunday school because my father's work as a drama and music critic kept him up late, so we went to the eleven o'clock service, and I was nourished by the great words of the Anglican liturgy, even when I didn't understand them, and leaned against my mother and daydreamed.

Sometimes the words of the minister would slip into my mind. Jesus left heaven and came to save us.

Save us from what? I wondered.

From our sinfulness. We are all born full of sin.

At Sunday dinner I asked my parents. "Are we all born full of sin?"

"We are all born full of possibilities of all kinds," my father said. "What we do with them is what counts."

"What about war? Is war sin?"

My father's mouth tightened. "It seems that it is inevitable." And then he started to cough and had to stop talking.

If Jesus was born two thousand years ago to save us, why haven't more things changed? Why is there still hate and misunderstanding?

Yes, I was allowed to ask questions, but I would have liked to ask far more than I did. My parents ate late, at eight, or were out at the theatre or the opera, and I had a tray in my room. I knew I was loved and didn't question our schedule which certainly was not the ordinary one. It was normal for me, because it was what it was, and I ate with a book in my lap, happy in my imaginary world, and didn't understand that in many households story was not honored as it was in ours. My parents read aloud to each other every night. Story. They read all the Dumas stories about the three musketeers. They read Dickens. They read the modern novels.

I was not part of these nighttime readings, but in the morning before breakfast I would beg my mother to tell me a story. "Tell me a story about when you were a little girl."

Her childhood was so different from mine it might have been on a different planet. My father's family came from New York and Philadelphia, but my mother was a Southerner, and after the War Between the States (yet another war) all anybody had left was story. People were poor; many of their houses had been burned; many husbands and fathers had been killed. But they had stories, and they told them and probably embroidered them, and my mother never seemed to run out of reminiscences of her childhood. All her friends were cousins, growing up together in a small Southern town, trying to make a new world out of the defeated old one. I was fascinated and nourished by my mother's tales, from the story of my great-great-grandmother who was the only friend of an African princess, to the cousin whose first job after graduating from law school was to find Stephen Crane's mistress, the famous madam. Later, when he learned that no black person could be admitted to a hospital, he set about raising the money and built such a hospital.

Because my mother grew up nourished and informed by story, she and her cousins were able to see needs ignored by those who had not been given the empathy that comes from the insights of story. Jesus told stories, and not everybody understood them. Why? If we understand the truth of story, we are more able to feel at home in the world of the Gospels, and to understand that the Good News is indeed good. Jesus' stories start with what is familiar (a woman who has lost a coin, a shepherd who goes out into the night after a lost sheep), and as we think about the parables we understand that the simple stories have far deeper meanings than we realized; they are messages for us. And it is important that we read them in the order in which Jesus told them. They are not isolated anecdotes. They follow the pattern of journey.

The messages of Jesus' stories were important for me. My parents' loving God was not sentimental; my father coughed his burned lungs; I was nearly eighteen before they burned away completely. Several times my mother was ill in bed with a nurse in a white starched dress tending her; I knew she was very ill but not what was wrong. I suspect it was yet another miscarriage; I was the only baby who made it through the nine months in the womb. But God was still a God of love who could be trusted.

In the outside world things were different. I was unhappy in school. One of the teachers scolded me for telling a story and it took a while before I realized she thought I was lying. Story was a lie! No. Story was truth.

I did not fit in that school. I was shy and awkward; one of my legs was longer than the other and whenever I was tired my knee ached and I limped.

I went home from the sterility of school to the real world of story, to my favorite books, written by George MacDonald and E. Nesbit and L. M. Montgomery and Louisa May Alcott and Frances Hodgson Burnett, books which cared about honesty and courage and truth. Books which affirmed for me that God is indeed love and came to live with us as Jesus of Nazareth because we are so loved. Children of God, God who didn't mind if we limped, as long as we were truthful.

One of my godfathers gave me a beautifully illustrated book of Bible stories. I read it and reread it, turning the pages carefully, reading the story of God's love which is gloriously true. With us it may be impossible; with God nothing is impossible. I never tired of God's stories. The truth of story was always fresh and, despite repetition, always new.

As a child it was easier for me to understand that than it was later when I knew more. The story of Jesus' birth has been oversentimentalized until it no longer has the ring of truth, and once we'd sentimentalized it we could commercialize it and so forget what Christmas is really about. It should be a time of awed silence, but it has become a season so frantic with stress that the suicide rate mounts alarmingly, and for some people death seems preferable to the loneliness and alienation of Christmas.

Somehow we've almost managed to kill the story, but not quite. It was still there for me when I was a child and slowly turned the pages of my beautiful Bible book. I loved the story of Noah and all the animals. God wanted to save not only the people, but the animals, too, for God made all the animals. They were different from people, but because God had made them, it seemed to me that they, too, were children of God.

I loved the story of Joseph and his wonderful coat and his jealous brothers and how, in the end, they all got together. But my most favorite story was Mary Magdalene seeing Jesus after the Resurrection and hearing him call her name and then knowing who he was.

And I knew that Jesus calls us all by name.

And Jesus was the God we call by name, God, a loving parent who transcends all our limited and limiting sexisms. In my Genesis trilogy I often use *el* (the earliest name by which the Hebrews called God) instead of him or her, he or she, and I find that helpful and, I hope, unobtrusive.

★ BEYOND THE SILVER HAIRBRUSH ★

CHAPTER 2

THERE WAS MUCH TO WRESTLE WITH AS I WAS growing up in New York in the twenties. Survivors of the war played frantically. Another war was brewing.

"Father," I begged, "there'll never be another war, will there?"

My father would not lie to me. He explained the lineup of the nations as mistrust grew in the Balkans. I did not want to hear. But I felt the breath of war like wind from the dark clouds on the horizon.

"But how can God let there be another war when war is so terrible?"

"God does not cause the wars. We human beings do."

"But why doesn't God stop it?"

"We are creatures with free will; God refuses to interfere with our misuse of it."

Thus began the continuing question of God's omnipotence and human free will. God gave away power when he made creatures with free will. That was a strange thought: God, who is all power, gave away power! And yet the ability to give power away, lavishly, lovingly, is greater than hanging onto power as human beings try to do. With us power is control. With God it is freedom.

So, then, if God has given us freedom, and if freedom is good, why is there so much pain? If Jesus came to save us, why do we still turn around and kill each other?

At bedtime my parents listened to the story of my day. If I had done something unloving or wrong I confessed it and was met with immediate forgiveness and hugs. Then, secure in their love, I would watch as they left for the theatre or the opera, my mother in an evening gown which smelled of her favorite fragrance, my father carrying his elegant top hat. They were glamorous as well as trustworthy. I learned more at home than I did at school, for I was not a successful schoolchild. I received little understanding from my teachers who did not like differences and who sided with the children who wanted someone to pick on.

At home I read and wrote in the privacy of my little back room. It was a long time before I knew that my parents often quarreled, and that their arguments were almost always about me and my upbringing. It was even longer before I realized that my mother's unconventional suggestions would have been better for me than my father's conventional ones, but my father always won. He wanted me brought up like an English nursery child, occasionally seen but not heard. They agreed on the "best" dancing school, but not acrobatic lessons.

Where was God in the twenties? War was on the horizon. My parents took tango lessons with a group of friends. My father coughed. My mother miscarried a little boy. The word *cocktail* came into the vocabulary. My father's many elder sisters were invited to lunch, and if my father heard about it ahead of time he vanished for the day. He went to his office in the Flatiron Building and worked, writing short stories, articles, plays, movie scripts. He could no longer do the traveling which had been his work as a foreign correspondent. He went to church and I was too young to understand the expression of pain on his face.

The world was uneasy. People worried about the drinking, the parties, the jazz, the changes the war had brought about. Things were not going to go back, be the way they were; Earth time moves only in one direction. Prohibition was voted in as a countermeasure to the search for pleasure. I listened to my parents talking and asked what prohibition was. It's a new law, I was told, to stop people from drinking alcohol.

I had heard the word *cocktail,* but I had been blessed in never seeing the abuse of alcohol. My parents had one drink and one drink only before dinner. It was a ritual for them, a time when they sat quietly together after the tensions of the day, and talked.

My father said, "Prohibition will make people drink more alcohol, and worse alcohol. Legalism does not make for moderation."

I learned later that his words were very true, but my parents were moderate. Jesus and his friends drank wine and I assumed that they were moderate, too. I still did not see very much of my parents, whose lives had a rhythm very different from a child's, but when they came to say good night to me at bedtime, they gave me their full attention. When they punished me, I knew that I deserved it. I didn't mind a smack with my mother's silver hairbrush. I did not resent it. I had done something wrong and deserved a reminder that it was wrong and should not be repeated. I most certainly did not consider the smack child abuse.

But a close friend of mine who was also smacked with her mother's silver hairbrush did consider it child abuse. It took me a long time to figure out why she considered the silver brush child abuse and I did not.

My parents were Episcopalians, but they lived in a wide world of the arts, theatre, music, painting. It bothered my mother that some of her favorite artists did not live exemplary lives, but that did not stop her from loving Mozart or George Eliot. When I did something that deserved spanking with the silver hairbrush I got a smack, followed by a hug and a kiss, and that was the end of it. What I had done was over and was not referred to again.

My friend grew up with parents who belonged to a rigid evangelical church. It was far more important that you live a virtuous Christian life than that you might write Beethoven's *Ninth Symphony*. When my friend did something that was considered wrong and the silver hairbrush was brought out, she was told that she had hurt Jesus. What she had done was not left alone after the smack with the silver hairbrush, but she was reminded over and over what a terrible thing she had done.

So, yes, in her case the silver hairbrush constituted child abuse. It is often not so much what we do as how we do it that makes the difference.

The punishment that was terrible to me was being forbidden to read for twenty-four hours. Once during this discipline I confessed that I had forgotten for a moment and opened a book. My mother did not seem to hear me, and she did not lighten my sentence. She was, as it were, not there. I was forced to realize that something was wrong, but I was not sophisticated enough to know what it was, or that I was part of it.

My parents fought over where I was to go to school. I had started in a small school that went only through third grade. My first little report cards were all that any parent could hope for. "As usual, Madeleine and Alexa lead the school"—Alexa, my first good friend, who has stayed in touch despite vast geographical distances.

For fourth grade a new school was found for me. Surely my poor report cards, on both the academic and behavioral side, should have told my parents that something was wrong. I went from the top of the class to the bottom. Everything I did left something to be desired. Why was I understood and encouraged in my first little school, and misunderstood and criticized in the new, larger one?

Alexa was in a different school, but one weekend I was invited to go with her to her family's country "cottage." Alexa came from a rich and notable family. The cottage was a mansion. But what I remember of that weekend was going for a solitary walk in the woods near the house. Alexa's uncle was spending the weekend at the cottage, and he came to me and began talking kindly. He sat on a log and pulled me onto his knees. Then he began to kiss me wetly. All I knew was that this was not right, and I slithered out of his grasp, though he grabbed at me; I ran. At first I could hear him following me, but I ran faster, and evidently he did not pursue me. When I got home I was able to tell my mother what he had done. She was calm in agreeing with me that his behavior was wrong, and told me I would never again be allowed to go to Alexa's for the weekend.

Another time I was sent to spend two hot July weeks in the country with friends of my mother, two women, and the daughter of one of them, a girl a couple of years older than I. I was not made to feel part of the family. The two women were polite, but they excluded me.

On the first evening I sat down at the table instead of standing and waiting for grace to be said, and was chillingly reprimanded. Since at home I ate alone on a tray in my room, my lapse was understandable. On Sundays when I ate with my parents after church we said grace. But my regular time to thank God was at bedtime when I said my prayers.

I mumbled apologies, and was not hungry.

At night in our bedroom the girl began to pinch me as a punishment for not being a good Christian and threatened terrible things if I screamed. Nevertheless, I told her mother, who said I was speaking nonsense and she would not listen to lies. The pinching continued, painful and incomprehensible. I was covered with bruises. When I got home after two weeks of misery, my mother certainly saw the bruises. I think I was reassured that I would never have to go back.

These are mild examples of abuse, but they were abuse. My mother's silver hairbrush was not abuse, but these were. They were abnormal. I was not permanently scarred by them, but I do remember them, and they give me a good idea of what abuse is like.

Alexa's uncle came from a secular society; the two women were "Christian." What made that man, important in the world of art, want to touch my prepubescent body? Why were those two women judgmental and unwelcoming? Why did the girl enjoy giving pain?

My childhood was full of ups and downs, insights and blindnesses. I did have more opportunity than many children for daydreaming, reading, writing my own stories. I believed in fairy tales and wee folk, and I knew that ultimately there had to be a happy ending. I clung to that because I knew that much in between was not happy. Jesus grew up in a small country where many freedoms had been taken away by the conquering Romans; if the Jewish people were not actively at war, they were still living in a country occupied by foreigners who had taken them over. I knew that there was something terribly wrong in a world of war, in Jesus' day, in mine. Why was I given a book at school that showed the "Huns" impaling Belgian babies on their bayonets? It left a terrible impression of terror on me. It was like Herod ordering his soldiers to kill all the children under two because he was afraid that a new baby had been born who might take away the little power the Romans allowed him to have.

It made even more terrible my father's words that we were moving toward yet another war. Why didn't Jesus stop war? Why did he allow people to hurt and hate? Even with these unanswerable questions I took Jesus and the love of God for granted, and it never occurred to me that this love did not cover the entire planet; God's love was as great for those in strange countries who had never heard of Jesus as it was for me who went to the Episcopal church every Sunday. It did not occur to me that anybody could put limits on God's love.

All that was being discovered in the world of science simply emphasized the greatness of the Creator. Science was never, in my mind, a threat. It simply provided new ways of telling the story and glorifying God.

I accepted mystery, and I knew that there was much I did not understand. That, of course, was one reason for growing up: to understand.

One day I was in the bathroom, standing at the basin, washing my hands. And Jesus was there. In the bathroom with me. Telling me without words that it was all right and there was work for me to do. I did not question his presence. It seemed very strange and embarrassing to me that he would approach me in the bathroom, because I was a private and rather prudish child. Why didn't he come to me in church? Or when I was saying my prayers? Or even in the park? Somewhere more appropriate.

Certainly I didn't tell anybody. I have never mentioned it

before in all these years. But I didn't forget.

One day there was a strange silence. In the apartment, on the streets. The stock market fell, plummeting downwards, wildly out of control. The Crash had come, blowing the remainder of the postwar world to shreds, as devastating as a bomb.

We were not as affected as many people, because we were neither rich nor poor. But everybody was affected. The entire Western world suffered. There were not enough jobs. There was not enough food.

I was nearly twelve.

When Jesus was twelve he slipped away from his parents and went into the temple and astounded the religious leaders by the depth of his questions and the answers he gave when they questioned him.

I had stopped asking questions, even at prayer time. When life became precarious at home the questions were no longer safe. By refusing to ask what was wrong, I was holding the fragile bubble of my world in my hand, protecting it by not questioning it, keeping it from shattering into a million fragments. I put myself into a state of arrested development by staying a child. But questions were being asked by others. Decisions were being made. I was not consulted. If I wanted to stay a child, my parents cooperated with me. My most coherent prayer was, "God, please make it be all right. Oh, Jesus, help."

Suddenly we were on a small ship sailing for Europe. The apartment where I had spent my first twelve years had been emptied, the furniture put in storage.

And so was I.

My father's health deteriorated. Places like Saranac, hospitals for people with sick lungs, were too expensive. What were my parents to do with a twelve-year-old girl while they were struggling to find a place they could afford where the air was clear enough for my father to breathe without pain? I was put in boarding school in Switzerland where I felt so alienated that I nearly lost Jesus completely. What I was being taught at school had nothing to do with what my parents had taught me at home. I knew that Jesus calls us all by name, but I could not hear the call in this cold school, English, and Anglican. We were taught good manners, moral rectitude, and strict obedience. Nobody mentioned Jesus. An Anglican clergyman came to the school and talked about the world of Jesus' day, but not about Jesus.

Where was Jesus?

Not in storage.

Sometimes I felt his presence when I had time (we were not allowed unscheduled time) and could look out the windows to Lake Geneva and the mountains of France. Jesus could walk on water. Like Peter I felt that I was drowning. Pull me up!

Sometimes I felt a small nudge. I thought I could hear Jesus whisper, I am still here.

After two years we came back to the States, to North Florida and my maternal grandmother, and her death.

And I woke up.

Storage had, in a way, been safe. But being alive was better, even though it hurt. I asked questions again. I knew that my grandmother was dead. Death had happened. And to my absolute surprise the world went on, ignoring this momentous event. We drove into town and through the crowded streets, and people just went about their business. Nobody knew that my grandmother was dead. Nobody noticed. I skipped her name that night in my prayers. In a pained voice my mother told me to keep her in. She was still alive, in Jesus' love. Jesus promised that our lives matter. Our deaths matter. Sometimes we forget. My mother taught me then to pray for the dead. I have never stopped.

Why should we pray for the dead when in Christ they have everything they need? I pray because my love of parents, husband, is still alive. Why should I stop praying for those I love? They are still part of my love in Christ. I prayed for my husband for the forty years of my marriage. Why should I stop now, as though our time together did not matter?

After my grandmother's death I was sent to another boarding school, but one where I was happy. I made friends. My teachers liked what I wrote. At the dinner table we sometimes talked about the various theories of the beginning of the universe—depending on which teacher sat at our table. Some of them were nervous about cosmic questions. Others were willing to discuss anything.

We were given great treasures outside the regular school curriculum. Every December we did three plays from the Chester Cycle, one of those great medieval dramas first played in the cathedrals in England. Because I was tall and spoke reasonably well I was usually cast as one of the shepherds or one of the wise men, while the girls with the best singing voices were the Red Choir, and the rest of the school dressed as peasants going to church on Christmas Eve. It was during these productions that I first heard Bach's beautiful "Jesu, Joy of Man's Desiring."

In the spring we performed a Shakespeare play out in the gardens, again living with great language and singing the beautiful madrigals of Shakespeare's day. One year the play was *Much Ado About Nothing*. I was cast as the monk/priest who helps untangle the complicated plot. Beatrice, one of Shakespeare's most delightful and witty heroines, spars verbally with Benedict, who will ultimately be her husband. She has a friend, Hero, who is engaged to Claudio, one of Benedict's friends. The villain of the play stages a horrid trick on his friends. He has one of the chambermaids dress up in Hero's clothes and come out onto the balcony at night, so that it looks as though Hero is having an assignation with someone other than Claudio. Claudio swallows the accusation without question, and his response is devasting. He allows the marriage ceremony to start as though all is well, and then he stops the proceedings and humiliates Hero in the most brutal way possible. At the end of the play, as usually happens in comedies, the trick is discovered. Hero is vindicated, and Claudio has forgiven her—for what she has not done—and the wedding continues.

One day after rehearsal I sputtered, "How could she marry that loathsome toad?"

That night in bed I suddenly thought of Joseph, and his tender love of Mary, even when he discovered that Mary was pregnant, and not by him. Claudio's reaction of unquestioning and outraged belief in Hero's infidelity is the opposite of Joseph's compassion. And I wondered whose reaction would be more likely today, Joseph's or Claudio's?

Two stories. Each one illuminates the other.

★ THE DIVINE INTERFERENCE ★

CHAPTER 3

DURING THE HOLIDAYS I WAS ABLE TO TALK WITH my parents. I wasn't afraid that what I was learning in the world of science in any way contradicted the Bible. No! It opened it up. My father said that despite the constant quarreling between science and religion, the religious establishment tended to live in whatever universe the scientists showed them. For a long time it was planet-centered, the rest of the heavenly bodies reverently circling us. Having our planet home displaced as the center of the universe was a terrible blow to the church but ultimately it had to be faced that we live on a little blue planet revolving around a middle-aged sun on the outskirts of one of billions of spiral galaxies.

My parents had been married nearly twenty years before I was born, and so they had been through the crisis of evolution, and it didn't seem to have bothered them much. I couldn't see why having creation on a divine rather than a human time table was so terrifying. Didn't God make time? Why did Darwin's theories create such religious panic? Why would a threat to a theory be a threat to God?

Did Darwin threaten the Bible, or only literalism? Doesn't the Bible say that God's time and Earth time are different?

My father explained that his faith was not reasonable because it wasn't for reason but for love that Jesus came, and whether God took a few days or a few billenia to make the universe didn't matter very much.

Why does it shake us so when something new and seemingly contradictory is discovered? How can we go on believing this if that is true? Our understanding of God changes and sometimes we forget that it is only our understanding that changes, not God.

Too often we try to fit what we believe about God into what we believe about Creation. For a long time the establishment tried to hold onto an omnipotent God who had created a predetermined universe where he (God was definitely a he) knew when a hen was going to cross the road, when someone in Greece was going to sneeze, when a snake was going to shed its skin, when Aunt Gwen in Maine was going to make apple jelly. God had written and completed the story. When it was believed that everything was already predetermined, from the beginning to the end, *free will* was more of an empty phrase than a challenging possibility.

If God didn't know everything, then God had lost power. No, no, not lost power, given power away in a loving act of grace. God is lavish with power, not grasping it, as we do, but joyfully giving it away. When God dared to make creatures with free will, God made us real instead of puppets manipulated by a potentate, and God's love was made greater than ever. And here we have another magnificent paradox: human free will and God's plan. God's loving plan for Creation will ultimately be fulfilled, God's will and ours working together.

How can we have both? God's plan and pattern and our free will?

The only analogy that makes sense to me is the writing of a book.

When I start a book I know what I want to say, where I want to go, what my theme is. I think about my characters, what they are like, inside and out. But, as creator of the book, I give my characters free will. They surprise me by saying things I didn't expect them to say, rather than what I had planned for them to say. They are frequently far better or far worse than I had thought they were going to be. Sometimes they make radical changes in the plot. But in the end the book is far more mine than if I had insisted on knowing everything ahead of time, keeping control of every little action.

So God does not lose control of the divine plan by giving us free will or by coming as Jesus to show us what that free will is really like. When Calvin's misinterpreters talked about predestination, they took away any idea that we might be made in the image of God, for surely the Maker is free! I still shudder for the little children who lived in terror because they were afraid they had already been damned to hell, even before they were born. What kind of a God would predamn or presave people? Was it something to do with divine omniscience—that there wasn't anything that God didn't already know?

"I believe that God knows all the possibilities," my editor said, "everything you or I could possibly decide or choose. Thus, every way we would choose would be within God's knowledge, but it is not determined."

That's a good way of putting it.

(Years later, my friend Luci told me that when she was a child she often lay in bed at night trembling with terror in case the Rapture came and her parents were taken but she wasn't found worthy.

Worthy?

Who is worthy?

What kind of a frightening God measures the worth of a small child and finds it wanting and offers no grace?)

There are a lot of Calvinists on my family tree, but I am not a Calvinist. And Calvin's theology might have been expressed very differently if he had known about Einstein's discoveries or Heisenberg's indeterminacy principle or the world of particle physics!

The struggle to understand continues. How much are we predetermined by our DNA? How much free will do we have? Psychologists argue about nature and nurture, and they both play a part in our development.

God's giving us free will does not mean indifference or impotence. When I listened to my father cough and was helpless to relieve his pain, I knew that he was dying and that his last few years in a draughty cottage on a beautiful beach far from any intellectual stimulation were darkly lonely, but I knew that God was not indifferent.

When Father talked about God he was looking at his own pain, his own mortality. The universe is so enormous and may be only one of many universes; how can we insignificant, stiff-necked people be a matter of divine concern?

But we are. Alone on the dunes at night I cried out in passion that we are. What else does the Incarnation, the divine interference, mean?

Wherever there is love, there is Jesus. Known or unknown, named or not named. Are there planets where people have grown up loving God and Creation and each other? Where religion binds people together instead of tearing them apart?

Despite all our present knowledge, how little we know. Recent astronomical discoveries indicate that there are galaxies older than our universe, and since that's astronomically impossible, then the universe must be older than it is, or older than we think it is, and that Word which spoke the universe into being is older than it all, and no age at all, since the Word was before time and spoke time into being for us.

Joy!

Christ, in being born as Jesus, broke into time for us, so that time will never be the same again.

My father understood that, even as he walked along the beach breathing the damp, salty air, trying to find healing for his burned lungs.

And then my father died. It was not a surprise. That the burned lungs would finally give out was inevitable, and they could not withstand that final attack of pneumonia.

I knew that for my father death was a release, and yet I knew that at age fifty-seven he was not ready to die. There was still a residue of the old *joie de vivre,* even when we talked about serious things.

I did not understand death.

Where was the church?

Not there. No help. There was a funeral, a burial. But no vital affirmation of resurrection.

"At least he's out of pain."

"At least he's not suffering anymore."

"At least he's happy now."

Happy? Where?

No pink clouds for my father, thank you, no golden harps. No red and burning hell, either, with little devils with pitchforks.

God.

Jesus.

I went through the last months of high school in a limbo of nonfeeling. Went to college. No one had told me anything I could believe about what went on after death. Were we still, even if in a different way, alive? Would the God who had come to us as Jesus abandon us when we died? Would we truly be put into the ground as a seed and, according to Paul, come up as something quite different?

I asked questions which were not addressed in any of my classes. I enjoyed my friends and teachers and tried not to let them see that I was deeply, darkly depressed. At last and unexpectedly I fell in love and finally wept. With the tears the depression dissolved and was replaced by a kind of faith which questioned but received few answers. Nevertheless, it survived, fragile, but there.

I wanted to understand. I wanted God. My mind baulked at the stupendousness of it all; only with my heart could I accept the infinite God becoming incarnate, enfleshed, human and divine. That's the tough one, human and divine. Both. Simultaneously. But that is the foundation of our faith. Christ has come to us as Jesus. Jesus was fully human and Jesus was fully God. Like Mary, I say, "How can this be?"

I don't know how this can be, but on it hangs the doctrine of the Trinity. Jesus' divinity comes from God and his humanity comes from his mother. If Mary and Joseph could believe the angel, why can't we? Does it offend our reason? Of course. It is totally unreasonable.

It is not that in believing the story of Jesus we skip reason, but that sometimes we have to go beyond it, take leaps with our imaginations, push our brains further than the normally used parts of them are used to going.

I majored in English literature with a smattering of the great French and Russian writers, and I had some superb professors. I wrote short stories, finally drawing on my own experience, mostly about a man and woman and their adolescent daughter wandering through Europe. I wrote more deeply about my parents than I knew. I started what was to become my first novel. I was through with the religious establishment, but occasionally my roommate and I would go to a small, French-speaking Catholic church because there, in that musical language, we found some mystery.

In the middle of the rational world of academe, I needed the scandal of particularity, God come to live with us, despite all our warring and sinning and refusal to understand.

I graduated and went "home" to New York and shared an apartment in Greenwich Village with three other young women and continued my search. There was an Episcopal church at the corner of my street, and often I would drop in, late at night, just to be quiet, and perhaps to try to pray. I did not go to a church service. I walked the streets of the Village with my dog. I returned to my little apartment and read. I lay in bed at night and read my great-grandmother's prayer book and understood that I had to let go all my prejudices and demands for proof and open myself to the wonder of love.

I read Schweitzer's *The Search for the Historical Jesus* and learned much from it: the reverence for all life; the uncomfortable fact that often we must make choices where there is no right choice to be made, and we must prayerfully make the choice we believe to be the least wrong, never forgetting that it is still wrong. But I learned very few facts about the historical Jesus. Schweitzer tells me more about Jesus in his recordings of Bach's work than he does in his writings, and I play those recordings frequently.

Throughout the years I have dutifully read many other searches for the historical Jesus. Sometimes the researchers have missed the point. They have forgotten the story. They have forgotten that story is true.

But we have the story as it has been told for nearly two thousand years, the story of a man who changed history in a way we have hardly begun to comprehend. When we have held true to the story it has been a life-giving one. When we have tried to control or manipulate or legalize it, it has been the cause of mayhem and murder. We do not own stories, and when we try to limit them, squeeze the life out of them, lose the love that gave them to us and fall back into that fatal human flaw, pride, hubris, we're right back to Adam and Eve who listened to the power of the snake instead of the creativity of God.

My friends and I sat on the floor of our little apartment to eat—for a long time we had no table—and discussed Pearl Harbor and evil and self-sacrifice and theatre and art and God and Jesus. We had graduated from college; we were in the world of grown-ups; we said sober good-byes to some of our friends who were being sent overseas with the army or the navy or the air force. I earned enough with odd jobs to pay my share of rent and food and worked on my first novel. In the evenings we gathered together to eat and discuss.

Despite the war, we felt excited and alive. I quoted my father's belief that despite the constant bickering between science and religion the Church's understanding of God is usually in the context of Science's understanding of the universe. There were few scientists in the world of Abraham and Sarah, though there were sophisticated astronomers in Egypt and had been for millennia in other parts of the planet.

"Stonehenge," someone said.

Someone else remarked that our primitive forebears were not as primitive as we have sometimes thought.

One young man in New York on leave, wearing his sailor's suit so that we could not forget we were in a world of war, scowled and said that the ancient Hebrews lived in a polytheistic world where they nevertheless understood themselves to be chosen by God as special people.

Circumcision was the sign of that specialness, and certainly was a sensible health measure in a desert world of little water and no daily showers.

"I take two showers a day now," someone said. "Once I get sent overseas, who knows when I'll see a shower again."

"You have to do it—"

"Take a shower?"

"Stop Hitler."

It was not an ambiguous war. If Hitler was allowed to take over the world, wipe out the Jews, we might be plunged back into the Dark Ages where the stories were kept alive only because the old monks with infinite patience copied out Scripture and other available writing.

We talked about Copernicus, Galileo, Bruno, with their radical visions of their universe, putting religion and science deeply in conflict. Bruno was burned at the stake because of his speculation that there might be different times for different planets. Why was this seen by the established church as a threat to Jesus? Galileo had to recant what he knew to be true, murmuring under his breath, "But it does move." Our growth in knowledge changed our understanding of the universe, but surely it neither changed nor threatened God. Yet it did threaten the power of the church and our place as the center of the universe. Could God love us as much if we were merely a planet in an ordinary solar system in a spiral galaxy, instead of the center of the universe?

To some people it seemed that the intimate God who loves us, knows us, blesses us, could not be great enough to cope with the billions of galaxies flying away from us and still have attention for us tiny creatures. But yes! Yes, our God is great enough to love us despite the enormity of Creation.

We post–Pearl Harbor kids needed to know that amazing love in our dark world of war, full of terrible bombings and the rumor of concentration camps. One evening a week I was one of many volunteers who taught English to refugees—intellectuals and artists—who had to leave Europe and Hitler's persecution because of their Jewishness.

Jesus was a Jew.

The U.S. dropped an atom bomb on a densely populated city.

Dropped a second bomb, equally, unparalleledly horrible.

And the next year I got married and the world changed, inner and outer, and questions deepened. Into what kind of a world were we going to bring our babies?

The opening of the atom and the world of particle physics changed everything we thought we had understood as radically as had Galileo.

If we do not live in a predestined world, does that take away from God's omnipotent power? No, no, it makes it all the more extraordinary! When God gave us free will, the Maker did indeed throw away power. When Christ came to us as Jesus, that was an even more radical throwing away of power. But that's what our loving God does! God throws away power over and over again, while we greedily grab for it. A lover wants to love the beloved, not to wield power, but to love, hoping that the love will be returned in the same way. When we are caught up in power we are not free, but in bondage to the power we have grasped. God is completely free because power has been laughingly thrown away in order that love may reign. The throwing away of power requires enormous power.

The all-powerful God who manipulates every event is like that Oriental potentate. When Lord Acton wrote that power corrupts, and absolute power corrupts absolutely, was he thinking only of human power? God's rejection of power makes me wonder.

And of course this is glorious paradox and I am barely beginning to understand it. Why are we human creatures so certain that our current religious or scientific theory is the right and only and correct one? When we look at our human history we have replaced theory after theory with new and more plausible ones. Many accepted theories at the time of my marriage have moved and changed. We too, moved and changed, going from New York to northwest Connecticut and a small village; we had children. The USSR put *Sputnik* in orbit and the U.S.A. put men on the moon and the world shivered with the chill of the cold war.

We took our children to Sunday school and they were taught that God loved them and they were to be kind to one another because that would please Jesus. We loved our little church.

During the week in the village school the children were taught to hide under their little wooden desks with their hands over their heads in case an atom bomb fell on them. People spent more time hating the communists than loving God.

At night after the children had been put to bed I would take the dogs and go outdoors and look at the stars and suspect that we human beings were as far from knowing the truth of the manner of Creation as we ever were, and that there were many more extraordinary revelations to come. How exciting it was to see our beautiful planet as viewed from the moon! I stood bathed in starlight and love-light and I prayed for Jesus to come into my heart.

On Sundays after church we would read the Bible to the children. They were bored with the glorious organ music of the language of the King James translation, but responded immediately to J. B. Phillips. Today I would read to them from Eugene Peterson's *The Message.* In his version of John's Gospel I was startled to read of Jesus' appearance to the disciples after the Resurrection. He blesses them with his peace. Then he tells them that when they forgive people's sins they are gone forever. And then, instead of the familiar, "Whosoever sins you retain on earth, they are retained in heaven," which has always bothered me, Eugene Peterson's version says, "If you don't forgive the sins, what will you do with them?"

I had the opportunity to ask, "Gene, how do you justify that?"

He replied calmly, "The Greek can go either way. I chose that way."

Thank you, Eugene!

Thank you, Jesus, for your unlimited forgiveness.

Thank you, Jesus, for being born for me.

The beautiful colonial Congregational church in the center of the village was also the center of our lives. There I knew for the first time truly Christian community. We really did love one another, with all our faults and flaws. That was the pearl beyond price.

But I missed the observance of the church year, beginning with Advent, and moving through the birth of Jesus, with all its wonderful stories; following the flight into Egypt and the return to Nazareth; the lost years of Jesus' story after his time in the temple with the elders, and his reappearance when he came to John for baptism. I missed hearing the parables in context, when he told them, and to whom; they change considerably as the first enthusiasm with which he was greeted changed to incomprehension and then antagonism. I missed the long thoughtfulness of Lent, and the dark of Good Friday, and then the glory of Easter. And finally the Ascension and the coming of the Holy Spirit. At that time in the Congregational church (now that we are United Church of Christ it has changed), we celebrated Christmas and Easter and that was that. There was no sense of the chronological movement of Jesus' story, from birth to Resurrection. I missed that. When I directed the choir we sang the church year; I just didn't tell anybody. We had Communion four times a year, and it was merely a memorial service. Once I asked the choir what it meant to them, and the response was *nothing*. For me it was far more than that. If we are all made from the same stuff as stars, then we are partaking of that original substance which Christ called into being.

I'm not happy with the Big Bang theory being called the *big bang*, because these words seem to feed into our world of violence, where the good guys are the most powerful and win with their force. I like to think of that beginning as the time when Christ quietly called all things into being, and although there is undoubtedly a great deal of violence in the formation of galaxies—like the violence of childbirth—it is not a matter of power and winning but of creating and rejoicing.

I was grateful that our new young minister at the Congregational church affirmed a God of love, that no matter what, God loves us, and that love was what gave birth to the universe, and, in due time, to Jesus, and our own small Christian community.

Our young minister told us that God counts the hairs of our head. God knows the names of all the stars, and our names, too. We were all, every one of us, even at our most difficult, worth the love of Jesus, who was born for us.

Is that a fact? we might have asked. It's beyond fact.

It's not that I can't be bothered about facts, or that I think they don't matter. My study is full of encyclopedias, all the reference books I collected in college, dictionaries, books of word origins, concordances, Oxford Companions; but when I have acquired all the facts possible I am still left with dozens of unanswered questions.

So were the rest of us.

"Why do the wicked flourish and the innocent suffer?"

"Will there be atomic warfare?"

"Why hasn't Jesus' coming made more difference?"

We sat in that minister's little study and listened as he smiled and told us that in spite of pain and unfairness, and all the horrors done in the name of Christ, he still rejoiced in God's goodness. He assured us that the Incarnation, the scandal of the particular, makes sense of all the seeming senselessness with which we are surrounded. He pointed to the Bible, open in his lap. The Bible tells, but it does not answer.

One of the older members of the group said, "Thank you, Jesus, for dying for me."

As the newest member of the group that day, I said nothing, but thought, yes, that too, there's no end to our thanks. But it's God being born, living a human life, who gets me through my days; it's the Jesus of the every day who leads me through the trials and tribulations that come to us all and that sometimes seem more than we can bear. It was the wonder of Jesus' being born for us that got my husband and me through the terrifying Christmas week when we thought our little daughter had leukemia.

If we concentrate on Jesus' dying only, it's like listening to the last bars of a Beethoven symphony and missing all the great music that leads up to it. It's like telling the choir to sing *Amen* without bothering with the anthem.

The Jesus who was talked about in church, in the minister's study, in our prayer group, often seemed to be dead.

Who are you? I don't think I know you.

The problem was that all my education taught me not to believe in the impossible. It was all right when I was a child, and believed in wonders and marvels and wee folk and talking animals, and trolls and witches (for I knew there was evil, too), and so it was not difficult for me to believe in God's love, God's love coming to us in person.

But as soon as I came to the age of reason and was taught to believe only in reasonable and provable things, the Incarnation was too much: it was impossible, and I could no longer believe in the impossible. I wanted to believe. I knew that if Jesus was nothing but a good rabbi (and there have been many good rabbis), then he did not enter my heart and guide my life. I celebrated Easter, of course, but I did not understand it. I was told that Jesus was God and Jesus was human and it did not make sense; it was a contradiction. I believed in God, who made the heavens and the earth and called them good. It was Jesus who gave me trouble. The Jesus I wanted to believe in was not possible. I could accept the miracles; ordinary human beings have on occasion done miracles. But Jesus, the Son of God? Jesus as God? Part of God?

I was stimulated and sometimes excited by conversations about

God, but they were theoretical. They did not explain death. They did not explain sin and evil. They did not explain Jesus or why the world kept right on being full of sin and evil even after he had come. The Jesus described for me did not live in my heart, because he did not seem strong enough to pick up hammer and saw and do a good day's work. I looked at pictures of a pretty man with curly blond hair and blue eyes, rather watery, and a weak, self-pitying mouth, and thought that the artist had forgotten that Jesus was born in the Middle East, that he was a Jew, that the Scriptures of the Old Testament meant a great deal to him.

Through the tenures of several ministers who followed that first young one who taught us about love, I was told of a Jesus who was even worse than the self-pitying one. Jesus had been separated from the Father at the Incarnation, so far that he saw the Father only as a tyrant who wanted to wipe out his creation, one minister informed us, and he would have done so, because of our wickedness, if Jesus had not begged the Father to forgive us and then been crucified for our wickedness. I did not understand. Jesus called his Father Abba, the intimate name of love.

I was told gently but firmly that I would have to learn about God planning to crucify his only Son because we human beings had become so wicked that only Jesus' death on the cross would pacify God's anger. I understood the wickedness. Surely we are all sinners. But I didn't understand the anger. I thought God loved us, despite all the things we did wrong. From the pulpit I heard about the Good News, but I didn't understand the Good News, because although it was good, I did not see it shining in our hearts and lives.

In my search for Jesus who would set fire to my life, I kept getting stuck on old literalisms. From the pulpit I heard that all those who had been born before the Resurrection would be excluded from heaven. They had been born before Jesus' resurrection redeemed all things, and so they would have to be left out. Certainly I was hearing theologically skewed concepts, and reading similarly bizarre teachings in books recommended by current magazines.

Didn't God make time? I wondered. Would God really leave Abraham, Moses, Isaiah outside the gates of heaven, never to enter because they had been born before Resurrection time? It did not make sense to me because it was not love, and God is love.

Having been excluded in many ways during my own life, excluded by my fellow human beings, I could not bear to think that God would be like some of my mean-minded teachers and schoolmates!

Much has changed since the early fifties, changed in seminaries as well as in pulpits. Some younger friends have found it difficult to understand that Christians really were taught some of the strange things I heard from various pulpits in those dark years after we had dropped the atom bomb and moved into the frightening world of the cold war. Seminarians were taught that God is impassible and cannot suffer. God is perfect, and perfection cannot feel pain. Seminarians were taught that they must never be personal in their sermons, must keep themselves out of their words, and never tell stories of what had happened to them and how it affected faith and actions.

In my heart I knew that God's promise was that our loving Creator would always be with us, all of us, caring about us and everything that happened to us. We were God's precious children, known by God (as the psalmist affirms in Psalm 139) before we were formed in the womb. So how could God possibly exclude Daniel and his three friends who had refused to worship a pagan image but remained true to God? How could David be excluded, a man after God's own heart even in the midst of his wrongdoings? Or the woman who had been ill for so many years with the issue of blood and whom Jesus had healed when she touched the hem of his garment? What about the exclusion of those people who had been an early part of the story and had no choice? the widow of Zarephath, Esther, Gideon? Wasn't what I was hearing from the pulpit a human interpretation of something known only by the Maker? Weren't people trying to make decisions for God instead of listening? Weren't they trying to make the unexplainable explainable?

I don't think this chilly theology is taught anymore, but once upon a time in an odd interpretation of arithmetic and time, it was. And I wrestled with it and walked under the stars at night, and I called out to God to love us, to be with us in our pain and joy.

Perhaps some people might choose to be excluded, though it seems an incomprehensible choice, but there may be some who are so sunk into sin that they don't even want to get out.

Many decades have passed. Seminaries have changed. Theology has changed and is, I believe, much healthier and more loving than it was in those strange years after we had been unwilling or unable to come to terms with the human horror of a war which included concentration camps and atom bombs.

Too many explanations don't explain, nor does focusing on God's anger at our terrible deeds instead of God's love and forgiveness when we repent and beg to be brought back into the loving community of all of God's children. Are not Christians the community of the Resurrection?

I try to think of the Resurrection as it would affect my father, as it would affect my grandmother; as it would ultimately affect my mother, my husband, myself. It seems that there has been a line drawn between heaven and hell, and the decision has largely been made as to who is going to be on each side. Who made the decision?

Various theologians? Doctors of law? It was too cut and dried. It took us away from being the image of God into being potential discards.

And were we looking for an inner image of God in ourselves or an outer one?

I thought about my children and how much I love them. Surely God loves us even more than we love our children, and that's a love so great it can't be measured.

I would go home after church and make our traditional waffles and milk shakes, and we sang grace and were grateful for God's forgiving love.

★ KING JAMES'S IMAGINATION ★

CHAPTER 4

I STILL WANTED SOMEONE TO EXPLAIN EVERYTHING
to me so that I could understand it, explain it all so there would be
no more painful questions.

I knew something was wrong with my own thinking, and I
continued to ask my minister friends all my difficult questions, and
they continued very kindly to answer them with all the good
answers they had been given in seminary. They tried to find facts
for me to prove their theology, but there are very few facts.

Facts?

We know that there was someone called Jesus who was crucified
about two thousand years ago, and that's about all we know as far
as historical facts are concerned.

Even in my confusion, I knew that I needed more than facts. I
tried to believe, but when I wrestled with theology I felt that I was
surrounded by a deep, dense fog through which I could not see.

My heart believed even when my mind faltered. I listened to my
heart and I wrote *A Wrinkle in Time* as an affirmation that there was

indeed light in the darkness with which I was surrounded. I wrote it for God.

When I had finished I was excited, because I thought it was the best thing I had ever written. I waited with anticipation for word from the publisher who had done my most recent book. She diddled and dawdled and finally said, "I may be turning down another *Alice in Wonderland,* but I'm afraid of it."

Most of the subsequent rejections were not that encouraging. Just the plain printed rejection slips without a personal word. It hurt. I had had six books published, overall with reasonable success.

After nearly a decade in the country, we moved back to New York and my husband's world of the theatre, and I had great hope that once I was back in the city of my birth, the city that was the center of art and music and literature, a publisher would soon see what I had been hoping to write in this book, and would say yes to it.

I've written before about the long struggle to find a publisher. I didn't know that mainline publishers did not publish science fiction. I did not know that science-fiction novels didn't have female protagonists. I struggled to keep on keeping on. I painted bright murals on the cupboard doors of the kitchen. Our children were in an Episcopal school so we went to the local Episcopal church for consistency's sake. My husband was steadily employed in the theatre, but like every actor I have ever known, when the play he was in closed, he was convinced that he would never, ever, have a job again.

But he did, and we enjoyed each other and our children and our friends and finally *A Wrinkle in Time* was published, and after that

I did not have the long months and years of waiting to hear from a publisher.

I began to get speaking engagements to librarians' groups, teachers' meetings, colleges, universities. I was invited to speak at Wheaton College, and that was my introduction to the evangelical world. It is amazing to me that I was in my mid-forties before I had even heard of the evangelical world, and I didn't hear about it until just before I left for Wheaton when the dean of the cathedral came into the library where I was volunteer librarian, and told me about it. I listened, open-mouthed.

But the moment I reached Wheaton I felt at home, and two of my dearest friends have come from that first experience, now over a quarter of a century ago. The evangelical world didn't seem to me to be much different from the Congregational church in northwest Connecticut, except it didn't have the New England reticence. By precept I was taught spontaneous prayer, and I will be ever grateful that when I am asked, sometimes out of the blue, to pray, I can do it, and without embarrassment. I felt loved and affirmed at Wheaton, and saw little or no conflict between this new world I was meeting and the Episcopal world I grew up in.

Wrinkle and its companion books were affirmed as "Christian" books, though I didn't then and don't now like that label; basically I don't like labels. And what is a "Christian" book? Is it something that will be appreciated and understood only by Christians? Is it telling the Good News to those who already know it? Is it preaching to the choir? I want my books to bring joy and hope and courage, and I pray that they are and will be inclusive and not exclusive.

Meanwhile my faith slowly grew. I just lived long enough to live through pain and joy and birth and death and failure and fulfillment; slowly I let go my demands for reasonable explanations. I lived long enough to grow old and believe, once again, in the impossible. The impossible is easiest for the very young and the very old. If I am blessed with continuing to grow old, the impossible will become less and less difficult. The impossible is all that makes life itself possible, with all the anxieties and griefs and pains that come with experience. Joy, too, I don't forget joy, but joy sometimes comes in the midst of pain.

Finally I understood that I had to believe in the impossible, rather than trying to prove it.

I can't prove anything that makes life worth living. My childhood, adolescence, young womanhood, my marriage, childbearing and rearing, loss of parents, husband, friends, all become comprehensible when they are set in the context of a love so great that in ordinary terms it is impossible.

I still don't love God or Jesus as much as I should, but I'm learning that my love of God grows through my love of people. My understanding that God forgives even my most base thoughts is deepened as I learn to forgive those who hurt me, sometimes deliberately, and most deeply when I need to forgive someone who has hurt someone I love. As one young friend said fiercely, "You can do pretty much anything to me, but touch one hair of my child's head, and you're dead!" I understand that if I do not love, I cannot believe.

Meanwhile, while I was growing, aging, while my children grew up, married, had children of their own, something else was changing in the world around us. It has always been a frightening world, but fear seemed to increase along with drug abuse and pornography. And I began to get angry criticisms of my writing, especially *A Wrinkle in Time*. Yet not a word of the book has changed.

Something else has changed. What?

Suddenly the Bible seemed to be an idol rather than the truth of God. I was asked, sternly, "Do you believe in Creationism?"

"Yes, of course, but was it Greenwich Mean Time, or Eastern Daylight Savings Time, or Mountain Central Time? . . . Doesn't Scripture say that God's time and our time are completely different? So why shouldn't the first day take a few billion years as we count time, and the second day a few more?"

Literalism is a terrible crippler. The combination of fundamentalism with literalism has sometimes encouraged slaughter in the name of Christ. I don't like to use the word *fundamentalism* in a derogatory sense, since I believe in the fundamentals, so when I was writing *Penguins and Golden Calves* I coined the word *fundalit*, a combination of fundamentalist and literalist. It is meant to be a descriptive and not a negative or unloving word. But there is no denying that the fundalit way of thinking has produced fear and anger and hardness of heart. In the fifties I could not understand some of what I was hearing about Jesus and God. In the eighties and nineties it was and is a different world, but some of the theology is just as confusing.

Why is *A Wrinkle in Time* now being censored as an unchristian and dangerous book? That hurts! How do I respond with love and without judgmentalism?

Imagination seems to have become a suspicious word for the fundalit. One group of women wanted the middle-school textbooks banned because they were afraid that these school texts might "stimulate the children's imaginations."

What?! I was totally baffled until I realized that in the King James translation of Scripture the word *imagination* is not used as we use it; it does not mean opening ourselves to wonder; rather it is a negative word.

> *In Genesis we read: "The* imagination *of man's heart is evil from his youth."*
>
> *Proverbs: " . . . a heart that deviseth wicked* imagination."
>
> *Lamentations: " . . . vengeance and all their* imagination *against me."*
>
> *Luke: " . . . scattered the proud in the* imagination *of their hearts."*
>
> *Romans: " . . . became vain in their* imaginations."

And so forth. Words change. Several translations now use the word *conceit* instead of *imagination.*

It is a mistake to assume that all words written in a translation several hundred years ago still mean the same thing today. What a sad loss it is to lose the current lovely meaning given to *imagination* and see it as something ugly! One small child at his uncle's burial watched the sky cloud over and rain beginning to fall, and said, "God is crying." How beautiful his imagination! My son was given a flashlight for his second birthday, and when there was an unexpected storm and the lightning flashed, he clapped his hands and said, "God's flashlight!"

When words change their meaning we must be careful to understand this, otherwise story gets changed along with words.

A senior monk was telling a novice that he had come to the point where it made no difference whether someone was king or beggar, sculptor or robber, but sometimes when he looked out and saw a stranger walking up the road, he couldn't help saying, "Oh, Lord Jesus Christ, is it you again?"

In New York, where I spend so much of my time, it is not always easy to see Jesus in those I pass on the street. In New York we tend to hurry along and not see anybody, much less see Jesus. In St. Luke's Hospital, across the street from the cathedral, the philosophy used to be that every patient was to be treated as Jesus. St. Luke's is no longer an Episcopal hospital, but I think there's still a residue of that old compassion. When I have been there as a patient it has been easy for me to see Jesus in the patience and humor of the nurses.

A patient in preparation for surgery must remove all jewelry, watches, rings. At this point my wedding and engagement rings have been on for so long that I cannot take them off even with warm water and soap, so they have to be taped. But many years ago when I was having minor surgery, I could still take them on and off, so I gave them to my husband for safekeeping during the surgery. When I was returned to my room, still groggy from anesthesia, the first thing I did was ask my husband for my rings. The student nurse who was in the room with us told me later that she would never forget my asking Hugh for the rings, and especially the expression on Hugh's face as he slipped them back on my finger.

Was Jesus in the room with us then?

Another time, not long ago, friends came to my hospital room to bring me Holy Communion, that glorious paradox of paradoxes.

Earlier that day I had been brought the *New York Times,* and the newpaper lay on my lap. During the wondrous words of the Eucharist my eyes dropped down to the picture on the front page, a picture of Rwandan babies conceived and born since the terrible troubles, because, said the writer, there was so little else to do.

The bread was put in my mouth, and the bread was for those little ones as well as for me and those who stood around my bed. Otherwise it was meaningless, and it is never meaningless, and it is never for myself alone. Here is the Love of the Creator shown in small things, a piece of bread, a sip of wine, a picture of some babies still so young that all they know is the comfort of their mother's breast, and the warmth of sunlight.

The winter of my foot surgery was a winter of special awareness of paradox. In New York snow fell on snow, keeping me housebound when I was not off on a speaking job. To add to the problem, my apartment is completely wheelchair inaccessible. There are corners and turns, and I could not get the chair either into the bedroom or the kitchen. When I could get to my cottage I felt free as a bird because it's all on one floor, with wide boards and no sills, so I could wheel around. I even mopped the kitchen floor from my wheelchair! And I wondered what was happening on the bitter nights to the street people who had helped me over the snowdrifts; where were they sleeping? The city shelters are always overcrowded, and in any case, unsafe.

Protected and warm under the old down quilt I had in boarding school, I tried to pray, simply opening myself to God and the love of Christ.

★A HORSE NAMED HUMPHREY★

CHAPTER 5

WHEN ETHEL HEINS INVITED ME TO BE PART OF A conference on the mythic in children's literature to be held in Dublin, Ireland, I immediately said yes, and then I suggested to my friends Barbara Braver and Luci Shaw that they join me in Dublin and that we go on to Iona and other holy places. To my delight they both immediately said yes!

Barbara (called Bara by Luci and me) took over the accommodations, using an excellent book listing Bed and Breakfasts. To her chagrin and ultimately our delight, she got the currency mixed up, reversing the order of dollars and pounds, reversing the exchange rate, and by the time her mathematical husband pointed out what she had done, the reservations had been made, and we stayed at much more elegant places than we had planned or expected. We gulped at the expense and then never regretted it. Every morning we ate full Irish/Scottish/English breakfasts (we all liked haggis), skipped lunch, and relaxed over dinner. I don't remember the weather, only our delight. Did it rain?

We talked, dreamed, prayed together. Everywhere we went we touched and were touched by the holy. We fell in love with the fields of sheep and the wonderful Border collies who herded them. We saw entire hedges of blooming fuchsia. In northwest Connecticut we're doing well if we can keep a hanging basket of fuchsia blooming for a few months. Here the hedges were radiant with spontaneous blossom. If Jesus had not actually walked the trails we traveled, perhaps Joseph of Arimathea had, for that is the tradition. In the very air there was a sense of the compassion of Jesus, his healing love, his demanding freedom. Each step we took reminded us of the scandalously particular love of God which sometimes we forget in the over-busyness of our daily lives. We were a delighted trinity, and we enjoyed the fact that during the time of our pilgrimage Barbara was fifty-six, Luci was sixty-six, and I was seventy-six. In our hearts there was no chronological difference, nor in our sense of the holy.

Bara and Luci came to join me in Dublin in time to make the trip to New Grange, where there is a temple which is five thousand years old, two thousand years older than Stonehenge and a thousand years older than the pyramids. The building is covered to protect it, but we could still see the opening above the entrance through which, on the winter solstice, the sun's ray pierces all the way through the temple to an altar in the center of the building. Whoever the people were who lived there five thousand years ago, they were astronomically and mathematically sophisticated, but this one building is all that is left of what once must have been a complex civilization. To whom was the temple dedicated? Whom did they worship?

I was particularly fascinated because about ten years earlier when my husband and I were in Egypt, we had seen a similar temple. It had been on an island that was going to be covered with water when the Aswân High Dam was built, so the temple had been moved, stone by stone, each carefully computed and computered, to another, higher island. This temple, like the one at New Grange, had been designed so that at the winter solstice the sunlight would shaft through the building to the altar. Different gods, a thousand years apart, but the same awe of the movement of the sun and the stars in their heavenly, patterned dance. The two temples were built with the same kind of astronomical and mathematical precision, as cultured as that of the twentieth-century engineers who moved the Egyptian temple to higher land. Does each civilization assume that it knows more than the ones before? Despite all the aid of our superb computers, the mathematics were fifteen seconds off at the moment of the winter solstice.

Why did that give me comfort? We do not always have to be right. What we did in moving the temple was nevertheless marvelous.

What is there in the human psyche that calls for a temple in honor of the Maker?

Bara, Luci, and I left our college dorm rooms in Dublin and the community of friends and colleagues we had found there, flew to Scotland, and picked up a car. The three of us were open for what each day had to teach us, the people we met, the villages, the narrow roads, the sheep, the dogs, the flowers. We tried to be open to the holiness of place, and we talked about the holiness of words. We talked about runes, those ancient collections of words put together at a time when words were understood to have power, power that came not only from the people who spoke the words, but from the words themselves. We can heal with words and, far more frightening, we can hurt. In so-called primitive societies today it is known that words can kill. Even evil thoughts can have murderous effects. We use words with both intents, either consciously or subconsciously.

I remembered one cold Sunday in New York when I wore my

warmest coat to church, with a pin on the lapel in the shape of a frog. As I came into the meeting hall, saying hello to people as I passed, a young man said, "That's an interesting pin."

"Yes," I agreed. "It was a Christmas present from one of my granddaughters."

"Isn't it a symbol of Satan?" It was more a statement than a question, and it shocked me.

"No!" I answered. "It's a symbol of resurrection."

"What?"

"It's a symbol of resurrection. The tadpole turns into a frog. The caterpillar turns into a butterfly. They are symbols of resurrection." I was still shocked. I think he was still unconvinced. But why on earth would he ask such a question of a fellow Christian, someone who came regularly to church, someone he saw every week? What was in his mind?

Words which hurt.

After the service a woman came to me and took my hands. "You were so kind to me last week. You put your arm around me and let me cry."

Words of healing.

Sometimes we are aware of the effect our words may have. Sometimes we are not. On our trip along the narrow Scottish roads, Luci and Bara and I found it easy to use the words of healing, opening ourselves to each other, knowing instinctively that we would not be misunderstood. We shared joys and griefs. We gave and received words of healing.

When I was starting to write *A Swiftly Tilting Planet,* I had the plot pretty well established in my mind, but I wasn't sure how to get into it or how to structure it. While I was struggling with this, I opened the day's mail and there, from a friend who was in Scotland visiting Iona, was a card with the words of "Patrick's Rune," the rune which was to be the backbone of my plot.

In this fateful hour
I place all Heaven with its power
and the sun with its brightness
and the snow with its whiteness
and the fire with all the strength it hath
and the lightning with its rapid wrath
and the winds with their swiftness along their path
and the sea with its deepness
and the rocks with their steepness
and the earth with its starkness
all these I place by God's almighty help and grace
between myself and the powers of darkness.

So there was the structure of my novel, come to me in the mail. I thought of those words often as we drove across countryside where runes and blessings and mysteries were still part of the air we breathed.

Spontaneously we were opening ourselves to the holy.

The way to Iona, our first major stop, led across the long, dark island of Mull. Why do I call it dark? It was a grey day, not quite rainy, not quite foggy, but with low clouds, making it seem later than it was. The road was the narrowest yet, a single-lane road so narrow that two cars coming from different directions could not pass each other, so every few yards there was a pull-over, a half-moon of space so that one car could pull over and the other pass. We drove along, all three of us feeling a peaceful quiet, where we could relax and enjoy our adventure and the stark beauty of the land around us without needing to talk.

After a while we realized that there was a tourist bus on our heels, tailgating us rather unpleasantly. Pushing. Obviously wanting to get by. We were going at what was a reasonable speed for that road, and there was another car in front of us. It was

Luci's turn to drive, and when she saw a pull-over to the right she turned off the road so that the bus driver could get by. In an instant he had slammed into the car in front of us, with a great shattering of the rear window, but amazingly little damage. It should have been a bad accident, but other than broken glass the car in front of us seemed unharmed.

Doors were flung open. Suddenly the bus driver's dark and angry face was thrust in Luci's window and he was shouting at her, blaming her for the accident, telling her that she should have taken a left-hand pull-over, not a right-hand one. On that tiny road it seemed that any pull-over which would allow another vehicle to get by was the one to take. But the bus driver kept up his angry accusations. We realized that in his rage the bus driver was willing to blame anyone and everyone but himself, and the fact that our car was not part of the accident seemed to increase his fury. His face was black with rage.

"It's your fault, my girl. You caused it."

Barbara, the diplomat, got out and began talking with the passengers on the bus. They were a group from the States en route to Iona, and Barbara actually knew several of them. They were very willing to say that the bus driver had been going too fast, that he had already driven a cyclist off the road, that he had been tailgating our little car. They were willing to sign a statement that he had been driving recklessly and unsafely.

The tour group said that they had hardly felt the bump of the accident. It was very strange. What should have been a terrible accident, involving our car, which was not touched, turned out to be amazingly minor.

I was feeling very shaken, but not physically. Before I had left for this trip I had had an uncomfortable sense of foreboding. I do not have these dark feelings often, and I have learned that they are not to be taken lightly, nor can I try to avoid them. I do not think

they are what is called prevision. They are not forecasting a predetermined future. When I had this same sense of foreboding when
my husband and I were in China, the cancer that was to kill Hugh
was already in his body. I was not concerned about something that
was not there or that had not already happened. I am not sure what
I was picking up on before leaving home. Certainly there is evil in
the world, and traveling in a strange country opens us up to
unexpected dangers. I had not told my traveling companions my
concerns; talking about them would have served no good purpose
and might even have opened more darkness.

We sat there in our car and waited for a replacement tourist bus,
for the angry bus driver had damaged his own bus; oil was leaking
onto the road. People chatted, Barbara soothed, but there was no
soothing the bus driver who wanted the world to know that the
accident was our fault, not his. His rage was like an ugly rain falling
on us all.

When the new bus came, we said good-bye to the people whose
window had been smashed, and they set off to find a garage. The
bus rumbled down the road, Luci started our car, and we finally took
off once more. In a low voice I said that I felt that we had been
spared from a fearful danger by some wonderful grace, and neither
Luci nor Bara laughed at me. They agreed that there was something
very strange about the accident, that it should have been far worse
than it was, and that our car should have been involved.

And the sense of foreboding left me.

It did not return. On that narrow road in Mull we had been at a
crosspoint of darkness and light, and the angels of light were there.
That is not an explanation, but it is what I felt.

As we drove toward the end of the island we tried to pray for the
bus driver, our words fumbling but earnest. We did not want to pick
up on the anger of the bus driver and let it get into us, which would
have been very easy. We tried to pray for a light of love which would

take away from his dark. He was, we agreed, trapped in some kind of evil, and we asked God to free him. And us.

We got to the end of Mull and parked the car and took out our bags for the ferry trip to Iona. It was good to be on the water, to feel the fresh sea breeze.

Once we landed we had a struggle to get our bags up the hill. We piled them into a waiting wheelbarrow, but it did not move easily and the way was steep. Finally we were helped by a kindly Scotsman and got to our hotel where we had simple, cell-like rooms which were full of peace and quiet.

In the long twilight we wandered around, and finally sat on the low, remaining walls of a ruined convent to say our Evening Prayers. We were not sure exactly in which century the convent had been burned, the nuns raped, everything demolished. This horror had not been done by some alien enemy invader, but by other Christians. It was horrifying to us that whoever was in power, Protestant or Catholic, felt that the demand to kill, literally murder, the other, was the will of God. We're still doing it, though perhaps in different ways.

This convent was so ancient that all feelings of horror were dissipated by the healing of time, replaced by a sense of acceptance and peace and God's healing. We said our night prayers and talked a little more about the afternoon's accident, again saying that we had been spared by a generous grace that transformed anger into compassion.

Jesus never stayed in anger, but moved into a tender compassion for those who wronged him. As he grew in years from childhood to maturity, from the bright twelve-year-old who awed the elders in the temple to the mature young man who returned to give his message of love, his understanding grew, too. His vision moved from one of exclusivity to one of inclusivity. What would he have thought of those who raped and murdered the nuns in this old convent in his name? The Christians who murdered Orthodox Christians? Not long ago I heard a very loving woman refer to someone as not being Christian, and then draw in her breath to stop herself; it was old Protestant training resurfacing. The person she was referring to was Catholic.

Jesus refused to wipe out. Even for the Romans, the enemy, the conqueror, he showed no hate. He did not hate those who were not Jewish, and when his own people turned against him, he did not hate them, he forgave them. Oh, yes, on occasion his temper flared. He let the scribes and Pharisees know what he thought of them. But the anger never stayed. Compassion did.

When that bus driver was pouring blame on Luci, surely he felt self-righteous. Wasn't he, in his accusations, participating in terrorism? Why do we need to feel virtuous? When I feel self-righteous, am I in the mode that can produce terrorism? Perhaps we have more compassion, more objectivity, in story, than when we think we have the facts.

Jesus was surprised that the church authorities felt outraged when he healed on the Sabbath, so outraged that they wanted to kill him. Surely their anger toward him was similar to the anger of the bus driver, whose face was so stormy it looked like a tornado. And didn't Jesus expect the elders who had been so impressed with him when he was twelve to listen to him with understanding now that he was a man? Surely their rabid anger was baffling to him.

When he told his first stories, didn't he expect them to be understood?

It was only after his parables met with resentment and rejection that he began to address them pointedly to those whose anger was as irrational as that of the bus driver.

Early in his ministry he told those who had come to hear his words, "You have heard it said, an eye for an eye and a tooth for a tooth, but I say to you that you shall not resist evil. But if someone smites you on the right cheek, turn your other cheek, too." Gentle, if unexpected advice.

Yet later on he said, "Woe unto you, scribes and Pharisees, for you devour widows' houses, and for a pretense make long prayer; therefore you shall receive the greater damnation." And their anger towards him was as self-centered and ugly as the bus driver's. It is an irrational anger that has not changed in kind since the people screamed, "Crucify him! Crucify him!"

In Iona we moved intentionally out of the noise of hostility into the quiet of compassion as though we were recovering from a severe illness. In the morning after breakfast we took a buggyride in a cart drawn by a horse named Humphrey. How could a horse named Humphrey not be holy? Clopping along through the stark beauty of the island chosen by Columba (Columcille) because from its summit he could no longer see Ireland, from which he had been expelled, we felt the holiness he had brought to Scotland, to this island. We felt his awareness that everything is holy because everything is of God.

In the afternoon Luci and Bara took a walk across the island. I did not go with them because my knee was painful, and so was my foot which was swelling hotly and hurting more each day. I would have slowed them down with my limping along, so I sat on a stone wall overlooking the water and wrote.

This land is holy
the sheep and the lambs
the abbeys destroyed
in the name of God
the remains of stone huts
for God-seeking hermits
the prayers of the nuns

still lingering like fog
despite rape and the fire
the sound of their voices
singing the praises
of God and the morning
the water for washing
the pots for the porridge
the fisherman's nets
and the sunset through raindrops
When we weren't looking
holiness broke through
bright as a rainbow

I sat on the wall, bathed in peace, listening to the quiet sound of the water. Tourist ferries came and went but did not break my solitude. There was no room for impatience or darkness of heart. Oh, Jesus, my Companion, my Guide upon the way, my bright evening Star.

The day after leaving Iona we drove to Lindesfarne, the three of us quiet as we traveled, thinking about what had happened, what had nearly happened, trying to see it as Jesus would have seen it. Being with two women whose faith was deep and strong helped me not only to strengthen but to articulate my own still-emerging faith. I knew that Jesus would have seen through the bus driver's hate to the brokenness that caused him to capitulate to the darkness within him. I knew that Jesus still sees through the horror to the unhealed wound that causes acts of terrorism.

What inchoate darkness was behind the torching of churches in the spring and early summer of 1996, churches attended largely by black people? This kind of racial hatred is incomprehensible. Do the arsonists think they are pleasing Jesus? Or are they simply sick people who cannot resist fire? Are they people who hate and fear those who are different? Do they actually think they are doing God's will? Hate has erased all the normal barriers. The burning of a church of any denomination is always suspicious (far too frequently arson) and cuts across religion and race. But this spate of one church after another breaks all statistics of hate and screams out the ghastly loss of the sacred. The powers of darkness seem to be closing in on holiness.

And yet how different is this from the raping of the nuns and the burning of the convent on Iona?

When I was a child, a church or synagogue used to be safe from vandalism. The sign of the cross was a protection against evil. Silver vessels and candlesticks used to be safe from thievery. What is happening to our places of sanctuary? Hate is like cancer, separate from the normal cells, devouring and not being nourished, annihilating itself along with everything it attacks. Hate is contagious. We asked ourselves how immune we were.

I told Bara and Luci of an evening newscast where it was suggested that what the world needed was not more prisons, but more churches. It was a strange and wonderful thing to hear on TV but, we asked, are the churches up to the challenge? The need is desperate. We must let go our rigidities and open up to the wonder that God so freely offers.

Luci, Bara, and I are all Episcopalian, but Luci grew up with the Plymouth Brethren and Bara grew up in the Catholic church. Many barriers seem to be falling away as our planet gets smaller and we learn more about what is happening in far-flung parts of the world. Certainly there were no barriers between us as we traveled and talked and prayed. We didn't have to understand every aspect of our faith in exactly the same way. It was enough that we knew that the Incarnation is God's amazing gift of love and we cannot explain it. When we try to explain it we lose it, as I discovered in my middle, rational years. I do not understand the Incarnation. I rejoice in it.

Lack of provable facts no longer bothers me. Theologians and philosophers and biographers have been arguing for two thousand years. From the Gospels we have a good idea of what kind of person Jesus was, and the Jesus who comes to me in the Gospels is far more exciting than the Jesus of many Sunday schools and sermons.

In a recent batch of mail I had a troubled letter from a young woman who believed that the Gospels indicate that Jesus totally denied the senses. What?

Read them again, I suggested. Listen to Jesus. He remarked that John fasted and wore camel's hair, and that he, conversely, was accused of being a glutton and a wine bibber. We know that he enjoyed eating with friends, relaxing at the end of the day. He healed the bodies and souls of ill and troubled people, and that's a pretty sensory thing to do. He had close friends, female as well as male. His first miracle was turning water into wine at a wedding feast, and he referred to himself as the groom, coming for the bride. He agonized at the thought of going to the cross, and begged that he might be spared this terrible cup.

No, I don't think Jesus denied the senses and their proper and legitimate uses. He was angered at the abuse of the senses, but that's a very different thing.

Now that I think of it, being born was pretty sensory. Was Jesus flesh and blood, as some of the early heresies denied, or was he energy only pretending to be flesh and blood? He was born a good Jewish baby, circumcised, brought up according to Jewish law. How on earth did anti-Semitism creep into Christianity when our God was born as an Orthodox Jew?

One of the books I remember from my freshman year in college is Henry Adams's *Mont St. Michel and Chartres*. After all these years the one thing that remains vivid in my mind is that the ordinary people in the Middle Ages living lives of great struggle turned to

Mary for comfort. Jesus had become so divinized by the church that he no longer seemed in touch with everyday problems. But Mary was not aloof, was a woman like other women, bearing babies as all babies are borne, in pain and hope.

I have never understood the fear some Protestants have had of the honoring of Mary. Why was she such a threat? Is it largely because a patriarchal society sees women as unimportant and unworthy? Did they want Jesus to spring, like Athena, from his Father's brow? Was the Incarnation too much for the reasonable male mind? Did giving Mary importance seem to take away from the uniqueness of Jesus?

One of the blessings of growing old is that I have finally moved past Thomas with his insistence on seeing the wounds to knowing that the wounds are there, for me, in me, in you. Perhaps it takes moving through a good deal of chronology to know how thin the world of facts is, how rich the unprovable love which made it all. What I believe in lies in the realm of love, not fact.

I was much more concerned with facts when I was forty than I am now.

Is the fear of Mary fear of Jesus' humanness, fear of the dual nature? Do we want to divinize him so that his divinity makes it impossible for us to follow in his footsteps, in his compassion, forgiveness, laughter? Is there something in us that wants a more unapproachable God? Or is it, yet, again, denigration of women? Women in Jesus' day were less than second-class citizens. Does love of his human mother elevate women to the position in which Jesus held them? Is the fear of Mary simply an aspect of the fear of women?

In the letter to the people of Ephesus it is written: "Before the world was made you chose us to be yours in Christ. . . . In love you destined us for adoption, as your children through Christ Jesus: such was your pleasure and your purpose." God's children. God's sons and daughters, affirmed by the love of Christ.

Christ Jesus. Wholly human. Wholly God. The two natures are bound together in love.

He was special even to those who failed to understand him and were frightened by him. We know from his words and actions that he was no weakling. He shocked his own family with his unconventional behavior. His sense of mission was passionate and he tried to elucidate it by telling stories, and even when he explained the stories to his friends and disciples they still didn't understand, and he wanted and expected them to understand. Sometimes it seems that the more he explained the less they understood.

He had a robust sense of humor. Many of his parables are jokes, told to put over a point. How many times can we hear a joke and still think it's funny? What's black and white and red all over? An embarrassed zebra. A newspaper. The responses are stale with repetition.

They no longer amuse or shock. We've heard Jesus' jokes too often. When he first told that story of the man with the plank of wood in his eye, wasn't it supposed to be hilarious as well as pointed? The more openly we read the Gospels, trying to listen to them freshly, the more we understand Jesus, and the more we understand how easily he was misunderstood. And the more we understand why he was feared.

What did Jesus fear? His very fearlessness antagonized the authorities. If you can make someone afraid, you have power over that person. Jesus' references to power were to the power of the Father, the Creator, something very different from human power which seeks to grasp, dominate, humiliate.

Is Jesus still feared today? Are we still trying to tame him? It doesn't work, then, or now.

Even when his immediate family criticized and misunderstood him, his disciples wanted to follow him wherever he went because they were utterly drawn to the brilliance of his love. But whenever they were tested they drew back in fear; it was too much. They were amazed at the unconventional people who were his dinner companions—lepers, and Romans, the occupying enemy, and tax collectors, who were even worse than enemies because they collected taxes for the enemy, keeping some for themselves. He even chose one of them as a disciple, one of the Twelve.

He chose the wrong friends, people who failed to understand him and who would abandon him in the end. He did his best to reach out to the people he grew up with; were they so familiar with him that they were unable to hear him? Scripture has given us hints that some of his friends and relatives thought he was crazy and so did not believe in his miracles, or in him. But Jesus continued his loving healing, his strange way of regarding people as though everybody matters. He enjoyed his friends, but they were strange friends, not the ones his family would have chosen for him.

Luke in his Gospel was very clear about what Jesus expected (and expects):

> *What you want people to do to you, do also to them. If you love those who love you, what credit is that to you? Even sinners love those who love them. . . . Love your enemies, do good and lend, hoping for nothing in return, and your reward will be great, and you will be children of God. For he is kind to the unthankful and evil. (from* The New Zealand Prayer Book)

What did his listeners think of that? Did they like it? Do we? Luke continues,

> *Therefore be merciful just as your Father also is merciful. Judge not and you shall not be judged. Condemn not, and*

you shall not be condemned. Forgive and you will be forgiven.

I need to hear and heed that over and over again.

In four short Gospels we have dynamite!

★ WHO KNEW HIM? ★

CHAPTER 6

JESUS CAME TO HIS COUSIN JOHN FOR BAPTISM.
Not surprisingly, John demurred. But Jesus insisted. His refusal to
set himself apart from other human beings was something his
disciples never understood. ("Yes, I have come to you as a human
being, I am the Son of Man. I am the One Who Was to Come. If
you knew me, you would know the Father. If you knew the Father
you would know me.") No wonder his disciples did not understand.
No wonder we don't, either. But aren't we told that faith is for the
things we don't understand?

There's much that I don't understand that enriches my life. I have
faith that every time I light the candles on the dining table and we
hold hands and sing, we are joining the angels. I have faith that
when I read Night Prayers with someone I love, this is a sacrament.
I have faith that my baptism matters.

I have faith that the baptism of Jesus was of the utmost importance, and so were the temptations—not only for Jesus, but for all
of us, too.

I've written about the temptations over and over again, but there's something new each time. We all know the scene, Satan urging Jesus to turn stones into bread, to jump off the highest pinnacle of the temple, to worship Satan with all his worldly power. On the surface it seems that Satan was tempting Jesus with power. But Satan was far subtler than that. God, who had given up all power to come to us as Jesus, would have found power easy to resist. What Satan was doing was tempting Jesus to retrieve power, to emphasize his divinity above his humanness, to reverse the Incarnation.

"Turn the stones into bread. Jump off the highest pinnacle of the temple. Show them that you aren't an ordinary human being like them. You are God! Aren't you forgetting that? You can play at being human, if you like, but you're really God. Show them."

Jesus was hungry. He had not eaten for forty days. He was exhausted and vulnerable. What seems ever more clear was that Satan was urging Jesus to deny the very reason he had been born of an ordinary human woman as an ordinary human baby.

How can we begin to understand? Christ, the Second Person of the Trinity, the Maker of all the galaxies, gave up all power so that this power might instead be human, mortal, finite, and that we might understand that this very humanness, mortality, finiteness, if we would only accept it, would be made divine, immortal, and infinite by God in the fullness of time.

We are again caught in an enormous paradox. If Jesus would turn the stones into bread, he would be divine, not human, and he would wow the populace. If he jumped from the highest pinnacle of the temple and the angels held him up, he would again be divine, not human, and everybody would worship him.

But Jesus held true to the promise of the Incarnation. Christ came to us as Jesus, a mortal, in order to show us how to be human, and he never gave in to the temptation to take the easy way out—no stones into bread. The relationship of Jesus to Christ, of Jesus to

God, the balance of divinity and humanity, has been confusing and confused for two thousand years. Jesus came not to be confusing, but to be a light to the world. His first disciples were fishermen, ordinary people, uneducated, yet willing to change their lives entirely to follow this extraordinary man. He didn't promise them earthly power; he spent a great deal of time chastising them for their eagerness for power, and this was something they never seemed to understand. Even at their last meal together the disciples were still quarreling over who would be the most powerful in heaven. Didn't they hear? (Don't we?)

Not then, not now.

Over the years my agent and I have negotiated with Hollywood regarding contracts for movies of my books, particularly *A Wrinkle in Time*. Not long ago I received a screenplay for *Wrinkle*. The first page was a normal title page. The second page simply had three words: *Love is power.*

I shook my head sadly. "He doesn't get the book. He simply doesn't get it."

Love is not power. Love is giving power away. Power in the sense of control. When our babies are little infants we have to use loving power to see that they are properly clothed, fed, have the right immunizations, are given love and cuddling and laughter. As they grow up we try to step aside, hoping we have taught them to make right and loving decisions. If we try to control or manipulate (and there are parents who continue to do this long after the children are grown) then we are not loving; we are using power for our own ends. There's a very fine line here and it's very easy to step over it:

power as love and power as manipulation. Thinking of Jesus and his calm rejection of power in favor of love is a help. Weren't the miracles power? Yes, but never just for power's sake. Never to prove a point. Never for Jesus to show off or to get his own way. And Jesus always attributed the power to God; it belonged to God and not to him.

When God made creatures with free will, that was a tremendous giving away of controlling power. When Christ came to us as Jesus, that was, again, a huge giving away of power. Whenever I love, I give away power. If I try to control or manipulate, then I am not loving, I am using power for my own good, even if I am convinced it's for someone else's good.

After he had rejected every one of Satan's temptations, Jesus went to Nazareth, where he had been brought up, and preached in his own home synagogue. He quoted the prophecy of Isaiah, and then told his listeners that that very day the prophecy was being fulfilled. But no one believed him, because they had known this kid all their lives. "Isn't he the carpenter?" they asked. "The son of Mary and brother of James and Joses and Judas and Simon, and are not his sisters here with us?" And they took offense at him.

Jesus said, "A prophet is not without honor except in his own country and in his own home." And Luke, the physician, has him add, "Doubtless you will quote to me this proverb, 'Physician, heal yourself.'"

What does that mean? What was wrong, that Jesus should say such a thing? Was it a fulfilling of Isaiah's prophecy about a man of sorrows, not beautiful to look on, but with wounds which were visible to those who saw him? It was of the utmost importance to the Jews that the age-old prophecies be fulfilled.

We don't know what the human Jesus looked like, except in negatives. He did not look like a Protestant or Catholic Christian, or an American. His skin was probably dark, as was that of his family and friends who lived under the blazing Middle Eastern sun. He probably had dark hair and dark eyes. But whether he was tall or short, whether his eyes were far apart or close together, whether his teeth in today's world would have been considered in need of straightening, we have no idea. We know that he had what today would be called charisma, or, more likely, chutzpah. He drew people to him by the joyous force of his personality, and his intimate closeness to the One he called Abba.

Abba, Daddy, Papa, Father.

Our mental image of the Father is often influenced by our fathers. I called my own father *Father* rather than *Daddy* or *Papa,* and that may have had its effect on my way of understanding the heavenly Father.

In many of my writers' workshops a common theme will begin to emerge. In a recent group the theme was overbearing, stifling fathers, who were particularly hard on girl children. There was a consequent lack of conflict in the stories, a reflection of, "Don't upset Papa."

Too often this repressive father is seen as a metaphor of the heavenly Father. But look at the Gospels! This isn't how Jesus saw the Father. This harsh Daddy whose power must not be contested is not the loving Father who cared about us so much that Jesus came to live with us, teaching us to love the One who made us. "Fear not, little flock," he urged. Tender. Compassionate.

Some of the fathers in the workshop were "men of the cloth," ordained men who were supposed to represent God, but who used their authority to wield power over their sheep, who had to be obeyed instantly and without question. No wonder the flock was afraid.

Jesus called us away from fear into love and truth, away from power into joy and compassion. He walked by the Sea of Galilee and he called Andrew and Peter, John and James, to come to be with him.

Together they went into Capernaum where Jesus healed a man with an unclean spirit, and the unclean spirit recognized him for who he truly was. It's amazing and awesome that the unclean spirits always recognized Jesus as the Messiah, even when nobody else around him did. Is it that unclean spirits still belonged to the spirit world, even though they were fallen spirits, and so were able to see where human eyes were closed? The spirits recognized the humanity and divinity of the One who banished them from those they tormented, for it is in the nature of evil spirits to torment.

They have always been around. They are here, now. In the bus driver on Mull. In muggers on our city streets. In irrational acts of shooting and knifing. Do the unclean spirits still recognize Jesus, now, two thousand years later? Do they still recognize and then reject him? They no longer flee into herds of swine. Jesus no longer walks the earth in human form as he did two thousand years ago. The Holy Spirit, the Comforter he promised to send, is here, and the unclean spirits are slashing at the holiness.

Were those around Jesus ever aware that the unclean spirits recognized the One Who Was to Come when they, themselves, did not? That the unclean spirits, unlike the Pharisees and the other religious leaders and the good, ordinary temple-going people, knew who he was? If so, Jesus' healing was all the more extraordinary.

But then, everything about him was extraordinary. The Sermon on the Mount was extraordinary, a sermon unlike any other sermon we have ever heard, and which was probably preached over many days. How much at a time can people stand of Jesus' radical turning things upside-down and inside out? Jesus gave them a freedom they had never known before. They laughed with joy. They listened with astonishment. They lived in a land of hierarchy, where power was eagerly sought, and yet he told them to be poor in spirit. Who were the poor in spirit? The beggars, the lepers, the women, the Samaritans, the nobodies, and he told them that it was the poor in spirit who would receive the kingdom of heaven. And that was just the beginning.

The Beatitudes reverse the normal order of thinking. He told them that they would be hated because of him, and yet they were to rejoice and leap for joy. He told them that they were the light of the world, and that they were to reveal the light, not hide it. And then, having knocked down the law as they understood it, he told them that he had come to fulfill the law, not abolish it. He told them that anybody who relaxed these commandments would be called least in the kingdom of heaven, and that their righteousness had to exceed that of the scribes and Pharisees or they would never enter the kingdom.

He told them that it is all right to grieve, to be meek, to be poor in spirit. Don't be afraid. Don't judge. If we judge, we open ourselves to judgment. Don't show off. Reject earthly treasures and earthly power. Keep the law. Love your enemy.

It didn't make sense. It was impossible. It was contradictory. He told them that the old law forbade them to kill, but that thinking evil of each other was murder, too. He told them that it was not just fornication but lustful thought that was sexually evil. He was fierce about the sanctity of marriage, and this was strong evidence of his compassion for women. Marriage was not, at that time, sacred. All a man had to say was, "I divorce you, I divorce you, I divorce you," and the woman was out. Since her husband kept all her property, she was sometimes out on the streets, because there was often no place else for her to go unless she had a loving family willing to take her in; and many had no one to care for them. Jesus' compassion for the plight of the discarded woman was profound.

His friends were ordinary people, fishermen, even a tax collector. He told them to come with him and they would, according to the King James translation, become "fishers of men."

When I was in college I read these words and wasn't sure they were compatible with higher education. But I needed them. My father had finally died and I didn't understand death. His death. Anybody's death. The world was dark and I stumbled along, bumping into spiritual and intellectual obstacles. Because being on the dean's list offered certain desirable freedoms, I managed to keep my grades up. But I felt lost. I went to church and nobody spoke to me and I felt alien and alone, so I never went back. What the old institution had to offer was no longer valid. There was war across the ocean. Killing. Hating. During the holidays I went to a dinner party where I heard anti-Semitic remarks to the effect that maybe Hitler had the right idea: look what he had done to improve the highways and the educational system.

Jesus was a Jew.

He was a good, observant Jew even though many Jews did not understand him and neither did anybody else.

He was a full human being, in contrast to some of the people around him with their petty snobbisms and downgrading of Samaritans (how many protagonists of Jesus' stories were Samaritans?), just as that man who thought Hitler might have the right idea was less than human.

And I, in my bleak depression, was less than human.

When Jesus made his blatant, radical statements the crowds were shocked, awed, relieved, delighted, excited. He knocked down the old, legalistic ways of thinking with something new which they could barely understand. He warned them about the folly of anxiety, and the evil of harsh judgment.

They followed him down from the hills and watched while he healed a leper. News of his healing powers spread, and a centurion came to him, asking him to heal his servant, who was gravely ill. A centurion was a Roman officer who was head over a hundred soldiers. He was part of the enemy. But when Jesus told him that he would go to the servant and heal him, the centurion said, "Lord, do not trouble yourself, for I am not worthy to have you come under my roof. Just say the word, and my servant will be healed."

Jesus marveled at the faith of this soldier, and this was the first indication that the Good News was for everybody, not just for any one particular group. It was for everybody who would listen and believe. And Jesus' mission was expanded, as it was when the Syrophoenician woman who had been begging him to heal her daughter reminded him that even dogs eat the crumbs that fall from their masters' tables.

This is one of the most amazing of the stories because it emphasizes Jesus' promise to be human, with all human limitations. He was brought up to be a good Jewish boy worshiping the great Jewish Jehovah, and he and his people were surrounded by other people who worshiped different and lesser gods, and who were therefore beneath them. He was taught to know and love Scripture and to believe that the prophecies were going to be fulfilled. The psalms were his familiar hymnal, and he would have known not only the affirmative, loving psalms, but the angry ones as well, and he would have been acquainted with Psalm 44 which begins,

We have heard with our ears, O God, our fathers have told us, what work you did in their days, the times of old, how you drove out the heathen with your hand and planted your people in. . . . For your people got not the land in possession by their own sword, neither did their own arm save them, but your right hand.

Did that psalm give the settlers in the New World the right to drive the "heathen redskins" from their homes? Did it urge the British to expand their empire? Who are the heathen? Those who do not know and honor the holy and undivided Trinity? Weren't some of Jesus' parables about heathens? Samaritans? lepers? others? What did Jesus think? Didn't God make everything, and all of us? Didn't God come to us as Jesus to call us all to be el's children?

That psalm has always bothered me. Do we feel justified and superior when we talk about the heathen? when we justified having slaves? Does it explain some of the centuries-old hatreds in Bosnia? Africa? the U.S.A.?

The Promised Land was already occupied. Was it all right to take it over because it was occupied by heathen? I don't know the answers to my questions. Is a group of Protestant soldiers raping a convent of Catholic nuns in Iona less or more heathen than the primitive savages on a far-flung island?

Jesus' choice of "others" as protagonists of his stories is all the more remarkable. In his human self he had a lot to learn and a lot to unlearn, and much of it must have been painful for him. He was far ahead of his time, as were the early abolitionists who saw that slavery was terribly wrong long before most good churchgoing people recognized it. There lies the impact of the Syrophoenician woman and her passionate request which gave the human Jesus the unexpected message that his mission was not just for Jews. And I am reminded again of God telling Abraham (in Genesis 12:3) "In thee shall all families of the earth be blessed." The message of God's love is for all the nations, for the whole world.

When we creatures were made with free will, the ability to make choices and decisions, God gave up control in a way so radical we have never quite understood it as we continue to strive for power. When God saw what a miserable mess we were making by clinging to power, Christ threw power away once again and came to us to show us that power was literally killing us.

So Christ left power and came to us as Jesus, to be our Redeemer. Christ our Redeemer: we say the words too glibly. What do they mean? How is Jesus our Redeemer?

If I sell a family watch to a pawnbroker, it has to be "redeemed." I have to return the price I received for it, and more. In the days when grocery shoppers were given green stamps they could be redeemed for some kitchen appliance, a blender, a set of mixing bowls. Redemption is a reminder that you don't get something for nothing. Jesus came to redeem us by offering his human life as the price, the whole life, from conception to resurrection. In the Beatitudes he tries to show us how we are to understand what he is doing.

Redemption has to do with Jesus' presence in our lives. It means that Jesus sees us as we really are, and loves us anyhow. Not only that, Jesus sees whatever is best in us, and by seeing it, brings it forth and continues to redeem us with his life, his pain and his joy, so that we have the possibility of becoming who we really are meant to be.

For years on our drive from New York to Crosswicks, my husband and I looked sadly at a once-beautiful old colonial house where almost all the paint had come off the clapboards. The sills sagged. It was a house in such terrible condition that we were afraid that one day when we drove by we would find that it had collapsed on itself. Instead, one day we found that the house had been bought, and we saw a family busy painting, hammering, bringing the house back to life and beauty. They had looked at the decrepit building and seen what it could be, and were remaking it into the once-lovely building that had nearly been destroyed by time and neglect. They bought the house and they redeemed it. The payment was love and labor as much as money.

That's not a perfect metaphor, but it helps.

Jesus sees what we might have been, and by being, himself, what we might have been and ought to have been but woefully were not, he offered us redemption by his very being. Dare we receive it?

Sometimes my husband and I would see a house which was once beautiful but which had gone *beyond* the possibility of rebuilding, was falling in on itself, with holes in the roof, broken windows, a house that was too close to collapse to be brought back to life. That metaphor would seem to reflect such human failures as child abusers or drug pushers shot to death by competing drug pushers. But here I am stopped by my absolute belief that God in his love is not going to abandon anyone. I am only one of God's stiff-necked people, so I do not know how God is going to accomplish this. If God has made us in the divine image, with free will, then God accepts our free choices. I have known parents struggling for years to find a runaway adolescent, to try to help a confused son or daughter turn away from drugs, to continue with anguish and prayer to do what is best for their most difficult children. And, as Jesus reminds us, we are only human parents trying our best, so how much better than ours is God's forgiveness and love and generosity. If I have need of proof that God is love, it is that God is still with us in all our sin and folly. Surely an angry God would have wiped us out long ago.

I saw another house that had been burned and was a horrifying blackened ruin as I drove past. Each time I drove by I saw the charred wreck and was saddened. Then one day I saw that the remains had been stacked together in a tidy but still terrible pile. Soon afterwards I saw the beginning of a new structure, and at last there was a clean white house with daffodils blooming around the door. It was spring, and I saw redemption.

Over and over Jesus shows us love and redemption. God thinks we are worth redeeming. Alleluia! O thou, most holy and beloved, my Companion, my Guide upon the way, my bright evening Star!

Jesus talked about houses. He told his listeners that those who heard his words and followed them were like a householder building a house on a rock, where it would withstand wind and rain. But those who heard his words and did not follow them were like someone building a house on sand, and when the storm came the house had no foundation, and fell.

Jesus told stories of warning and he told stories of encouragement. The good shepherd goes out into the night after the lost sheep, out into the rain and wind and dark until the sheep is found, and he carries it home rejoicing.

This is one of the loveliest of Jesus' stories, but evidently some of the ninety-nine good sheep resented it. Why should the shepherd just go off and leave them all in order to find the bad sheep who had left the fold?

That was more or less the view of the elder brother who resented the party the father was throwing for the selfish and spendthrift prodigal son when he returned home.

Jesus assured those who followed him of the love of the heavenly Father, which was so much greater than theirs. "If your child asks for a fish will you give him a serpent? And you're only a fallible human father. How much more does the heavenly Father love you!"

When Jesus told his stories he was often misunderstood, so misunderstood that the very people he came to save with his deepest love were the first to turn against him. It may not have been because they did not understand him as his disciples did not understand him, but that they understood him too well. They couldn't stand his having turned everything upside-down and inside out. It threatened their power which was held in balance both by the Roman overlords, and then by their fellow Jews. Because of their insistence on the law, the letter of the law, their power depended on keeping everything right side up, everything in its proper box, put on the shelf in the right order. If they let him turn things inside out it would be the end of their power. So they began to hate him.

He was surrounded by throngs, but how many heard what he actually said, rather than what they expected him to say?

Who is he? they asked each other.

They found only paradox and contradiction. If we think of Jesus as the Son of God as any young man is the son of his father, we anthropomorphize. Perhaps because we are human beings, that is inevitable, is the only way we can understand. But it is far more than that. He is the Son of the One who created the stars in their courses, and yet, as Christ, he was Creator of the stars and without him was not anything made that was made. We will never understand with our finite minds that, yes! he shouted the magnificence of the universe into being, and yet, as Jesus, he left this fiery home and came to our little blue planet as an ordinary mortal.

Everything is more than it seems, and we get occasional glimpses, revelations, but when we try to analyse and explain them we lose them. Angels were his chariots, and he rode upon the wings of the cherubim, and he is further away from us than galaxies billions of light years away, and he is as close to us as the beating of our own hearts.

He is with us because of a love beyond our comprehension, and it is only through our own love that we are able to know him at all. And it isn't even our own love; it is Jesus' love, expressed through us.

So what has happened to us?

Why are we not alive with joy?

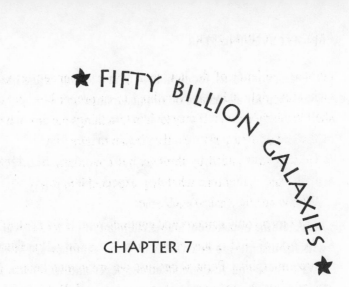

★ FIFTY BILLION GALAXIES ★

CHAPTER 7

JOY COMES OFTEN WHEN IT'S LEAST EXPECTED:
When a family member arrives safely, after having driven through a major snowstorm; when an unexpected piece of music comes on the radio, music that is tied in with a time of happiness; when I am kneeling at the altar with a friend. And I thank you, Jesus, for being born for me, for living all the way to death and dying for me because you were willing to be a mortal human being. And thank you for defying death by your resurrection, and for assuring us that as you went through life and death for us, you are calling us into the resurrection life with you. Thank you for leaving the glories of the galaxies and coming to us as one of us.

One of us? And who is us? We are, you and me, and the street people, and the farmers, and the executives with their briefcases, and the fourteen-year-old girl carrying her baby, and those who work hard to support their churches. And, oh, yes, the pagans and the junkies and those on the other side of the planet and the atheists and the searchers and . . . and . . . All of us.

Thank you, Jesus, for coming to us and loving us and healing us. Thank you for all that we do not understand.

Jesus left the amazement and excitement of his healings and went with his disciples to Peter's house. Peter's mother-in-law was sick with a fever and Jesus rebuked the fever and it left her and she immediately began to cook and serve them a meal.

Where was Peter's wife? Since she is not mentioned in the story it seems likely that she had died, as women so often died early in those days, frequently in childbirth. As far as we know, none of the inner circle of disciples, none of the Twelve, was married. They were young men, free to follow their Lord.

That evening, fulfilling the prophecies of Isaiah, Jesus continued to heal the sick and the lame.

In the morning, long before the sun was risen, he went to a lonely place where he could be alone with his Father and pray.

And here we come to another paradox, another upside-down-ness. We refer to Jesus as the Son of God, but Jesus referred to himself as the Son of Man, the son of us mortals for whom he had come, and I think we need to pay attention to what Jesus called himself. For this is the great mystery. Jesus who was mortal, Jesus who was God.

Jesus, who was seldom recognized by the mortals he came to save, and who was recognized by the demons he rebuked, is an eternal paradox. There is no separating his two natures, for they were his simultaneously. But in steadfastly referring to himself as the Son of Man, he was referring to his promise to be human for us, human all the way. He not only resisted Satan's temptations, all of which were to reject his humanness and do something magic and flashy, but he refused every temptation put in his path to drop his mortality and show himself in terms of Satan's false perceptions of divinity. Satan left heaven because he did not understand God; he knew only his own pride. And so he kept tempting Jesus with his own faulty understanding which stopped him from being either human or divine.

Once again I struggle with the extraordinary nature of Jesus, Jesus as God, and Jesus as the Son of God. How can that be? What does it mean? Jesus is Lord, Jesus is lover, Jesus is judge.

If Jesus was the Son of God, how was he the Son, when he was also God? When he called himself the Son of Man (man generically, male and female) he meant what he said and he wanted us to understand. Literalism is no help here. Nor is futile speculation about his mother with either fear or overadulation. Jesus' conception was not a case of heavenly fornication. It was not the way it is with human sexuality. Again it is mystery expressed in paradox. It is our story, an amazing story. It is the only way to tell the untellable.

The magnificence and magnitude of God's love are beyond our powers of comprehension but not beyond our faith. When I read various scholarly articles about the facts of Jesus' birth and life, I find myself unmoved. The Incarnation is so far beyond our factual comprehension as to be laughable. No number of Ph.D.'s will help us to prove it in academically acceptable terms.

What we are doing now in our attempts at inclusiveness has produced even more confusion. I am for inclusiveness, for understanding that God pronounced Adam and Eve to be male and female, made in the image of God, each different, each wonderful, each essential to the full image of the Maker.

Recently I read a book which suggested that Mary Magdalene was one of the apostles. This radical idea was met with such horror at the beginning of the nineteenth century that it had to be repressed. A woman as an apostle! The idea repelled, terrified. But neither could a woman in those days be a physician or a lawyer or most of the things that women today take for granted. Why is this speculation about Mary Magdalene such a horrifying idea? From what we have been able to learn it seems quite likely that she could have been one of the apostles, and she was surely one of the leading figures in the early church. It's not unimportant that Mary Magdalene was the first person to whom the risen Jesus appeared.

The dominance of Mary Magdalene has been underplayed because the female of the species was not thought of as *Sophia* (Wisdom), much less *Hagia Sophia* (Holy Wisdom). Women have been denigrated and put down by the masculine world, kept in their "proper places," whatever those were.

If this attitude is changing, if we wake up to the fact that Jesus' mission was as much to women as to men, that his attitude toward women was unheard of in his time, are we not changing our image of God and of the human race as having been made in the image of God? An outer image? Surely not! We can change what we believe to be the image of God, and have been doing that for thousands of years, but God has not changed, only our vain attempts at final definition.

If we change our understanding through our attempts at definition, we will also radically change the church institution as it has continually evolved over the centuries. There comes a moment when all institutions need changing, but such change is inevitably fraught with danger. It can be disastrous as well as creative, and once we admit that change is needed, we are open to both possibilities. It is not merely a matter of switching the emphasis from male to female, but of acknowledging both, of helping each to love the other, to marry, as the prince and princess must do in the fairy tales, so that we have the wisdom and intuition of women and the intellect and reasoning of men, and all the mixes that come with both.

As I read and reread the Gospels it becomes more and more clear that this is what Jesus calls us to do and to be.

Perhaps a lack of understanding of this vulnerable kind of marriage is what causes so many human commitments to break down. As I look back on my own forty years of marriage I am realizing only now how amazing my husband was for his time, willing to try to work out the balance of true partnership. Not that we always succeeded, but we did try, not by mathematical balance, but by love and understanding. We discovered quickly that neither one of us wanted to be the dominant one or to have controlling power over the other. Wielding power is not love but is, indeed, a kind of sadism.

Hugh was a wonderful father and we were blessed that our ideas of how to bring up our children coincided—that was a great gift. I am ever grateful that we were not like my parents with all their conflicting ideas about child raising! Hugh and I believed that love with discipline should be first and foremost. We didn't think much of the prevailing permissiveness, where the child was allowed to express any feelings without curb. We were severely scolded by progressive friends who told us that it was old-fashioned of us to try to teach our children to be courteous.

But we firmly believed that love and permissiveness are not the same thing. We had to love our children enough to say no.

Politeness for us was a form of loving, not formality, but courtesy. You don't stop saying please and thank you when you are married.

Jesus was not blandly permissive, with others, or with himself. His life was an example of the balance of action and rest. When he had healed many people of illnesses, he needed to be quiet and pray, pray that he might have the strength to be incarnate.

When I get overbusy and overwrought I try to follow Jesus' example and take time from all the unimportant little things that are making demands of me, and go off to be alone with God.

Like many of us, I am impulsive, and often with the best will in the world. I want to make everything all right. Sometimes I am given instructions in dreams. I am told to stop running and rest. Told that many of us are too quick to respond to requests for healing. We are so eager to help that we rush in with our words, our hands, our touch. Wait! Jesus told me in a dream. Wait until you are certain that God has come into your hands before you place them on someone for healing. It must be God's energy flowing through your hands, not your own. Wait. Wait. Until you are sure it is God.

Yes.

My dog, Doc, a golden retriever who was an affectionate, bouncy ball of love, used to come with me to the library of the cathedral and sit quietly under my desk, controlling her friskiness, lying at my feet without restlessness until it was time for a run in the yard.

One day a young woman came into the library to ask me for prayer for the healing of terrible pain in the bones of her jaw. We sat, a foot or two from each other, and I tried to wait until I knew that God had come into my mouth and my hands.

Doc quietly got out from under my desk, sat in front of Naomi, raised her paw, and put it gently on Naomi's knee and kept it there. This is anything but typical behaviour for a golden. Their love is usually ecstatically active: enthusiastic pawing for attention, wagging tail, eagerly licking tongue with little sympathetic kisses of love. But Doc sat there in front of Naomi, her paw steadily on Naomi's knee, without moving, quietly and steadily looking up at Naomi. I think we slipped out of time. I don't know how long Doc sat there before she finally dropped her paw and slid back under my desk.

There was no question in either Naomi's or my mind who had been chosen as the instrument of healing that afternoon. It filled me with an awed humility. We descendants of Adam and Eve tend to want credit for all such deeds, but God made all things, all creatures great and small, and all can be used for healing—or for destruction, if we are deep into pride and sin. What I felt was an amazed sense of gratitude for God's love, and a humble joy that in witnessing it I had been part of God's healing power.

Isn't it interesting that someone's over-high blood pressure can literally be lowered by stroking a dog or a cat? The animal is not consciously acting to lower the blood pressure; nevertheless it has been statistically proven that this is what happens. My own relationship with my animals has taught me much about playing, loving, healing. My little white cat does not like to hear voices raised in anger. When my son, Bion, was young, our old collie would not let anyone strange or in any way threatening go near our little boy. Animals have a sensitivity that we have forgotten as we have fractured God's love for all of creation in our greed, our grabbing for control, our prideful centering on the human creature as the only thing of importance in the created order.

Lately there has been a renewed interest in the power of prayer, in healing, in touch. We are learning to be patient, to understand that when we reach out to touch someone in prayer, our human hands do not possess the power but are momentarily given blessing by the Holy Spirit if we are willing and humble enough to be used.

In several books on prayer I have read that we Westerners are often too quick, too demanding, unlike the Easterners who take more time with prayer, who are quieter, who have more peace and selfless tranquillity. In many ways this rings true; in the Western world we have become a very mechanistic society. But then I wonder: why is it that Easterners are so much more sophisticated in their torture than we are? I am old enough to remember my friends returning from the Western Theatre at the end of World War II, often physically wounded, angry, horrified at the blind and brutal killings of war, but still, somehow, recognizable as themselves. But those returning from the Eastern Theatre were often so shattered in spirit that they were no longer the people I had said good-bye to months or years before. Some were trembling, terrified shadows of themselves. Some had withdrawn their essences into a lost vacancy. I am old enough to remember this personally; what has not actually touched our spirit is more easily forgotten, or unrecognized.

Why this difference of quiet depth in spirituality, and sophisticated brutality in torture?

Is it that we Westerners, especially those of us from the New World, are still adolescent, that we have not had the time to refine torture? And was the horror of Oriental torture the other side of the coin of peace and prayer uniting with the infinite? There is much to learn here that I have not yet learned.

A friend of mine, a beautiful and talented woman, was attacked from behind, thrown to the ground, and her face wildly and repeatedly smashed against the pavement. A woman unintentionally turning her car so that her headlights fell full on the victim caused the man to drop her and race for safety. He was, however, apprehended, and had committed other horrendous crimes, brutally mugging and in some cases killing young women. He admitted that this violence was what aroused him sexually. And yet there was found in his possession a book on Buddhist prayers of quiet which he claimed to be one of his deepest influences. How can this darkness and light go together? There is a skin-prickling obscenity about it, although I have been told that Oriental spirituality does put darkness and light together, seeing no contradiction.

I have watched with awe my young friend valiantly refusing to be a victim, through many surgeries, inquisitions, pain of mind and spirit and body. She has taught many of us important lessons.

Would there be as much violence on the streets if we paid more attention to the old values? I understand and share the concern of the religious right that we have tossed away our moral values, that there are no restrictions. Our devices and desires are like rivers in flood, losing their banks and roaring out of control. How can we set limits that are creative and not destructive?

The moral and social boundaries that were still in place when I was growing up are gone, often replaced by destructive and ulti-mately self-destructive behaviour. Self-fulfillment seems to be the ultimate aim, at no matter whose expense. Why is the divorce rate now well over 50 percent? Don't we take marriage vows seriously anymore? Jesus came to free us from the rigidities of the law, but not from being responsible for our own actions.

A friend of mine sent me a clipping from the Associated Press saying that Bishop James Stanton of Dallas is worried that the church is allowing itself to be reshaped by culture rather than the other way around. He brings up a legitimate question. Do our religious beliefs change culture, or does culture change what we believe? Or is it a combination of the two? Surely what we believe, individually, and in our institutions, is affected by what is going on in the world and by what we learn about the nature of the universe. Our understanding of God should be different now than it was when the church totally and solemnly believed that God had set Planet Earth in the sky as the center of all things, with the sun, the moon, and the stars circling docilely around us, and all for our benefit. We didn't give up the centrality of Planet Earth in God's concern for a long time. There are enough problems here to keep God busy. How can even the Creator keep in mind hundreds of billions of galaxies and all the possible solar systems and planets within them? It is more than we can even begin to comprehend, so much more that the response of some people has been to drop the idea of God entirely; we are alone in a hostile universe.

It is strange that the discovery of the enormity of the universe has produced less consternation among the religious leaders than Darwin and evolution. At least evolution was still centered on this one small planet. The idea of evolution would seem to contradict Genesis less than the enormity of the cosmos. The story is bigger than that of one planet with night and day, oceans and land, plants and trees, all creatures great and small. And yet doesn't Genesis imply all of that, too? It is not Genesis that boggles our minds, but the idea that our one dearly loved home planet, such a tiny part of the great beginnings, is significant in God's concern.

What did Jesus think of all this? From the Gospels, he doesn't seem to have been particularly concerned. Such concerns were not part of the culture in which he lived his human life. And didn't he, as God, make it all? What mattered to him was what went on in our hearts. What mattered was that we be right with God. What mattered was forgiveness, God's loving forgiveness of us, and our forgiveness of each other. Jesus was not attracted by people who were more worried about other people's sins (that mote in the eye, that stone in the hand) than their own love of God.

Jesus wanted people's hearts to change, but I don't think he suspected how radically he was going to change them!

The established church (of all denominations) does not like change. Change is frightening and tends to breed violence. In the early centuries of the Christian era people killed each other over the Arian heresy. In the Middle Ages people were burned at the stake because of the shocking idea that our planet might indeed be a planet circling a middle-aged sun among many suns in our galaxy. Then we had to gulp and accept that there are many galaxies. To the fundalits this may seem a heresy because it contradicts Creationism, Earth made in six days, and no older now than the generations listed in Matthew and Luke would indicate. Count them, from Jesus to Abraham to Adam, and you know exactly how old the planet is! But is that the only mathematical equation? Is that all there is? How does God count, and why would it be in human numbers?

Not so long ago the redeemed Hubble telescope detected fifty billion hitherto undiscovered galaxies in a slice of space no bigger than a grain of rice. Awesome!

Someone asked me with a certain incredulity, "Do you mean those new galaxies actually enlarge your faith?"

Yes, though I understand the question. It's all too big and we're too small. How can God possibly keep track of it all? In a universe with both the macrocosm and the microcosm too immense for us to conceive, how can we believe that God cares about each one of us, that the fall of the sparrow is noted, that even the hairs of our heads are counted?

Those new galaxies promise me pattern and order and a Creator not only great enough to make it all but to keep track of it all. I need assurance because I am concerned by the valid question the Texas bishop asks. Are we dominated by our secular culture, or does our faith in God help us to see things as they are and, perhaps, as they ought to be? And is our secular culture with its chaos any worse than the fundalit culture tightening the tourniquet around our moral values so that the blood is cut off? The secular culture with its soft, self-centered permissiveness makes me shudder, but so does the rigid self-righteousness of those who spend more time looking for that mote in someone else's eye than in helping to take it out and heal the eye. We all have motes, if not planks, in our eyes, and we need help and forgiveness instead of cold condemnation.

I think again of the bishop and his concerns which are, indeed, my concerns. But his solution to it all was to try to start a heresy trial against a retired Episcopal bishop who, a good many years ago, ordained a homosexual to the diaconate. From what I could read and hear, the heresy trial came from self-righteous condemnation rather than love, or a desire to help, or even to understand. Hate, it appears to me, is the heresy. We're still looking for the mote in the other person's eye. We're still ready to throw stones with the intent to kill.

Do we want to have faith in Jesus, or do we want to have the faith of Jesus?

And why this obsession, which has been creeping up on us, for what goes on below the waist? I want to know what is in the heart and mind. I want to know if a minister loves God, and cares about truth—not fact, truth. I want to know if the leaders of our churches are shepherds who will take care of the flock, who will be there for their people in all the tragedies and joys of life. I want to know by their actions rather than their words that our leaders love Jesus. I want them to affirm and love and be friends with the people Jesus chose. I want them to be able to laugh and rejoice and love with the whole of themselves—body, mind, and spirit.

Meanwhile let us try to pray as lovingly as possible, clumsily but earnestly seeking God's will. Even those who do not believe in God are tentative about prayer, sometimes even asking for it. It seems to be a matter of reasonable acceptance that people who are prayed for heal more quickly and completely than those who are not. I have been the beneficiary of many healing prayers and can witness to their efficacy. I have known of the prayers, but the amazing thing is that prayers are effective even when the person being prayed for is unaware of them.

★ DO YOU WANT TO BE MADE WHOLE? ★

CHAPTER 8

TWO YEARS AGO MY RIGHT KNEE, WHICH HAD
been painful and troublesome since I was a small child, finally had
to be replaced. At least that was the opinion of several respectable
doctors, and I was getting so painfully lame that it was apparent that
something had to be done. I sailed through the surgery and the
aftermath, resting confidently in the prayers which were sustaining
me. All went well. My friend Marilyn came all the way from Niles,
Michigan, to help care for me . . . not the first nor the last time she
has come to the rescue. My friends from the cathedral came
regularly through the snow to bring Communion to me. One of my
glorious memories came on Palm Sunday when my friend Canon
Susan Harriss came with Communion, and somehow or other
(angelic instructions?) we found ourselves reading the entire long
Palm Sunday liturgy, and we were part of all that went on during
that terrible and holy day, and chronos became kairos and we were
part of God's time.

All was well.

The physiotherapist was delighted with my amazingly rapid progress. "You're way ahead of schedule," he announced triumphantly.

And then, about six months later, something went wrong with my right foot, the foot on the leg with the knee replacement. Foot and ankle swelled up like a balloon, and were hot and feverish and painful. Tendonitis? Why?

I went to the rheumatologist who had the foot x-rayed. The x-ray was ambiguous, so she asked the surgeon to have a look at it. He was too busy. He couldn't be bothered. He said, "Oh, her arch has just collapsed. Tell her to go to Dr. So and So and get an orthotic."

Obediently I did as he suggested, but the arch was not the problem. The problem was that the knee had been put in straight as an arrow, and my body is not that straight, and my foot could not support the very straightness of the new knee. The stressed foot began to get more and more out of shape, hurting more and more with every step. I limped around in misery for a year and a half, the problem increasingly painful and undiagnosed.

Finally, I went to an osteopath who had helped a friend and who helped me. He sent me to another surgeon who immediately ordered a battery of x-rays. It turned out that I had been walking around with a snapped tendon and two broken bones in my foot. No wonder I was in pain! I know exactly when the tendon snapped, a year earlier, because I heard it, though I did not know what I was hearing.

The osteopath and the surgeon agreed that surgery was imperative.

I knew I couldn't continue on as I was, but I said, "I can't do it for six months. I have to give people that much notice."

The surgeon said, "If you wait, it will be much worse. You need the surgery right now."

I asked, "Can I keep my commitments from a wheelchair?" And was told that I could.

So on February 19, 1996, surrounded by prayer, I had the surgery.

In our own small ways most of us have witnessed miracles of healing; sometimes they have been miracles of selflessness, when we have truly listened to someone else. Listening is one of the greatest of all healing instruments, not listening with self-consciousness, but with complete focus on whoever needs to unburden grief or sin or betrayal. And then, usually, we are exhausted and need to go for a quiet walk alone.

I saw this after my foot surgery when my friend Marilyn once again came to stay with me and take care of me and, incidentally, take care of all the people who dropped in, including two who came to stay for several nights for reasons of weddings or meetings or whatever. I could see her getting more and more emotionally exhausted, and finally I would see her putting on her jacket and going out and walking until she was refilled enough to come back in.

One of the many things I had to learn during the months I was limited by a heavy cast was to accept being dependent, to accept that there was very little I could do without help. I kept my commitments in a wheelchair, which made travel even more complicated than it is normally (and that has become complicated enough). Ten days after the surgery I flew to San Antonio, Texas, where I was met by my friend, Betty Anne, and her son, David. Madeleine, wheelchair, and luggage were too much for one person. In the "olden" days my friends' care of me would have been called "acts of super abrogation." I did not realize how much I was asking of people in my attempts to keep my commitments until I was in the middle of it all.

In mid-May I was still in the wheelchair, having traveled through Texas, Michigan, Indiana, and North Carolina. None of these commitments could have been managed without great preparation by and with friends. I quickly learned to have deep sympathy for those who will never be able to leave their wheelchairs. I am in utter awe of the friends who made my travels possible. While I was in the midst of it, my incarceration seemed horribly long, but I knew it was going to come to an end, and I could look forward to walking again. Someone pointed out that I did not mention pain in connection with the surgery. I had been in so much pain for so long that a little bit more for a short while was hardly noticeable.

Should I just have canceled all my commitments and not have burdened my friends? I'll never forget Marilyn's making a game of tossing my folded wheelchair like a discus into her van.

And I'll never forget people who came to me with pain of body and spirit far worse than mine.

In our own lives and the lives of our friends we can understand Jesus' need to leave everybody and go off alone to pray, and we need to take heed of his example, and not feel guilty when we follow it. Most of us don't leave our busy lives and return to God often enough. My daily quiet time is in the evening after my bath when I sit in the big chair in my quiet corner for Scripture reading and the gentle service of Compline, where I can hold out the day to God for healing.

Even Jesus did not get the opportunity to be alone with God often enough, because people followed him wherever he went, clamoring for miracles.

After he had prayed one early morning in Capernaum, he left for Galilee, saying, "I must preach the Good News of the kingdom of God to other cities also, for I was sent for this purpose."

As he went about loving and caring and healing, his fame spread. He stood by the Lake of Gennesaret where the fish had been few and told his friends to let down their nets for a catch, and to their amazement their nets were filled. He did many miracles, and cast out many demons, and warned everybody not to tell anybody who he was.

Who was he?

Yes, yes, he was a mortal man, and he was God, and if nobody understood then, it is not surprising that we still don't understand, for this is one of those marvels that is impossible with us, but not with God.

Jesus was called to respond to a woman who had been taken in adultery, and who was cowering in terror as a group of men stared at her with condemnation and, perhaps, eagerness, looking forward to inflicting on her the traditional punishment for adultery: stoning to death. And they looked to Jesus to confirm the verdict.

Had he ever been told that his mother was pregnant before she was married?

Jesus took a stick and wrote in the dirt. What did he write? It has been suggested that he wrote the name of the man who had been the woman's partner in adultery. He wrote in the dirt twice, and we are given no hint in Scripture as to what he wrote. But he said to the crowd, "Whoever is without sin, let him cast the first stone."

Did his writing in the dirt have something to do with the crowd's response of shame, of their slowly drifting away? When they were all gone he told the woman that he did not condemn her, but that she was to "go and sin no more."

Perhaps our sins are less spectacular, but that story reminds me that Jesus did not (like some of the good people around us, then and today) condemn her. Jesus tells us to stop whatever it is that we are doing that separates us from God, from Jesus. From the whole Trinity. In *The New Zealand Prayer Book* the persons of the Trinity are referred to as Earth Maker, Pain Bearer, Life Giver, and that touches me deeply. Jesus, our pain bearer, bears our sins and our sorrows by coming to be one of us, Adam's sins, Samuel's, David's, those of the men who would have liked to throw the first stone and the woman who had been caught in the act (though not alone).

If we truly live in a universe can we ever separate ourselves completely from the sins of the whole world? I do not believe that we should wallow in false guilt about wrongs over which we can have no possible control. We cannot go around bent under the sins of our ancestors, but we can try to prevent them from being repeated; we can learn something from them. We can respect rather than shun people who live in different cultures, whose diet is totally unlike ours, and who are understandably still suspicious of us because of the wrongs we have done them in the past.

Knowing that we ourselves have no right to cast the first stone, we can have compassion and understanding of the sins of others, no matter how alien to us they may be. And we can pray for equal forgiveness of our own sins.

What would Jesus write in the earth today?

O my bright evening Star, my Companion, show me the way, show me the way.

Some scholars with high reputations see Jesus' healing of non-Jews as being anti-Semitic. It doesn't read that way to me. Jesus was a Jew. He wanted his own people to understand him. When he first started his mission he thought the Good News was entirely for the Jews. The other regions around them seemed to have no concept of a Messiah, the One Who Was to Come and heal all things. I think that it surprised and saddened him first that his own family could not understand, nor his friends and neighbors, nor the elders in the temple who had been so kind to him when he was twelve but who now did not understand the glorious message he brought.

He was a good Jew brought up to respect the religious establishment, an establishment he loved. Some of his healings of people who were not Jews came almost by happenstance: the centurion's servant, the Syrophoenician's daughter. Perhaps it took the human Jesus a while to understand that he had come to the whole world, and it was a much smaller world then than it is today. Not only was it planet-centered, but most of the people in the Middle East knew nothing about China, India, Australia, or the New World of North and South America.

Jesus' amazing message widened slowly, and the marvel is that it is now heard all over the planet, whether it is accepted or not. And whether it is distorted or not. Sometimes I hesitate to use the word *Christian* because it has come to mean so much meanness and narrow-mindedness and hate, with promises of vengeance and retribution and name calling. I'm not sure what *secular humanism* is, nor that strange thing called the New Age, but neither using fear as a weapon, nor condemning the current culture is helpful in changing it.

I seldom turn on the television news because good news is not news and I see no reason to burden my mind and spirit with a load of horror. But once when friends were visiting me, we turned on the evening news and we listened to a story of the emergence of a new group of terrorists, teenagers or even preteenagers who steal, rape, and kill with no conscience, no remorse, no sense of responsibility except to their own whims and fleeting desires. One young teenager was interviewed; he had a mouth full of gold teeth; he wore gold chains. To him a murder was justified if it meant he could buy another gold chain. How terrifyingly sad that he has lost all awareness of the value of life. I shudder with grief when I see the dead body of a fawn at the side of the road, or an egg that has fallen from the nest with the unhatched little bird caught in the broken shell. Life is infinitely precious.

Perhaps it was Jesus' sense of the preciousness of all life, of the infinite value of a sparrow or a child or an old woman, that made people follow him wherever he went, up a mountain, listening to his stories, calling for help, trying to find the magnificent life that was like a light around Jesus.

And Jesus, giving them life and light, needed to get away from the crowds and be alone with the Father. It is important for all of us. When I am at the cottage it is easy. I just step outside, toward the west and the mountains. Sometimes finding our wilderness is difficult, but it is always possible. In the city I have discovered that a subway, at a time when one doesn't have to strap-hang, but can have a seat, is a good place to tune out and be quiet.

The word *burnout* had not been heard of in Jesus' day, but he avoided it by going off alone. As John Greenleaf Whittier expressed it, he went away to the calm of the hills,

> *W*here *Jesus knelt to share with thee*
> *the silence of eternity*
> *interpreted by love.*

God's work is done better if periodically we leave all that we think we have to do and go off quietly to be with the Maker so that we can be refilled with the energy needed for the work of love. One of my problems, as I suspect it is for many others, is doing too much without giving myself enough time to be with God. Time to be with God is essential in order that our work may indeed be God's work, not ours. Sometimes I think of myself as a very small car turning into a gas station to be filled with faith.

One time when Jesus was exhausted (healing takes great energy), he got on one of the fishing boats and lay down in the stern. He was asleep when a heavy storm came up, and his disciples woke him in terror, telling him they were about to drown, and there he was, sleeping! Didn't he even care? He quieted the battering of the winds and the wildness of the sea, and the implication was that if we only had faith, we too could work in collaboration with the natural world God has given us. But most of the time we do not honor God's creation and so we separate ourselves from it, from all that God has made, and that is a terrible loss.

Why is it that some Christians are separating themselves from nature, seeing nature as a lesser aspect of creativity, rather than following Jesus' example? One explanation that has been given to me is that some fundalit Christians believe that God has given us exactly enough of the earth's bounty to last until the Second Coming, and since the Second Coming is imminent, it's all right to use everything up, air, oil, forests, land, because after the Second

Coming we won't need them. There's a strange selfishness in this. Where did the idea come from, anyhow? I do not believe that it is scriptural, and the smug greed in it frightens me. Should we not tenderly tend the land, and perhaps especially so if the Second Coming is near?

After the healing of the sea, Jesus healed a man of horrible demons and sent the demons into a herd of pigs which rushed into the sea and drowned, to the horror of those who tended the swine for the owner, and the joy of the man who had been released. And yet again the demons were the ones who immediately recognized Jesus as the One Who Was to Come.

He returned to Capernaum, and a paralytic was brought to him. The crowd was so great that the paralytic's friends took tiles from the roof and let down the paralyzed man that way—wonderful, loving, innovative friends. They were not going to be deterred in their desire to have their friend cured. But then Jesus shocked everybody by saying, "My son, your sins are forgiven."

But was it so strange? Centuries earlier, when people came to Epidaurus in Greece for healing, they had to stay in rooms outside the gates before they were allowed into the holy precincts where the priest/physicians were. They had to wait until their spirits were made clean enough so that they were fit to be healed. Is that so very different?

Jesus asked, "Which do you think is easier, to say 'Your sins are forgiven,' or 'Take up your bed and walk.' But that you may know that the Son of Man has the authority on earth to forgive sins, come, rise, take up your bed and go on home."

We tend to be most impressed with Jesus' telling the man to get up and walk, but our physical health avails us little if we are bent and burdened by sin.

I think of the man at the pool in Bethesda, where there were five porches, in which lay many people who were ill or lame, and who were waiting for the angel who, at a certain season, troubled the water. Whoever was first into the pool was made whole of whatever disease was causing pain and anxiety. There was one man who had been there for thirty-eight years. Jesus asked him, "Do you want to be made whole?"

Do we want to be healed? Of our diseases, our anger, our resentment, our hurt feelings? Before we can be healed we have to let go of whatever it is that is holding us back. Sometimes we are unaware that we are holding onto something, a disease which may make us feel important, an anger that we have been unfairly treated, a guilt that keeps nagging at us. The man replied to Jesus, "There is nobody to put me into the pool when the water is troubled, and while I am trying to get there, somebody else is always ahead of me."

Jesus said, "Get up. Take up your bed and walk."

And immediately the man was cured, and got up and walked.

Once again, this happened on the Sabbath. The man was asked who had cured him but Jesus had immediately slipped away into the crowd and the man could not answer. Later, Jesus saw him in the temple and warned him. "You are cured of your affliction, but make sure you do not fall into sin again, or something worse might happen to you." Had the man not entirely let go of whatever was holding him back?

Doctors today are learning that a healed spirit may make the difference between life and death. There may be two cases of equal severity, but one patient will recover, and the other will die.

Our immune systems are great mysteries, no matter how many vitamins we take to reinforce them, no matter how many psychiatrists we consult. I believe that laughter is good for the immune system, but so, indeed, may be tears. If we do not grieve for loss and pain at the appropriate time, our immune systems are going to feel the lack. But not everybody who gets flu during an epidemic has a depressed immune system. My husband's illness came during one of the happiest times of our marriage, when we were giving readings together which were so successful we had more invitations than we could accept. Our comfortableness with each other was deep and warm. We were happy. And then, out of the blue, cancer struck. And killed. Hugh was surrounded by prayers. He was only seventy—that seems young, to me.

I don't need to understand miracles now in the midst of my human life. I have to believe that what happens to us will be used in God's plan for the universe. We are again tangled in the contradictions of human free will and God's will, but ultimately God's will indeed will be done.

After Jesus had healed the man by the pool, the religious leaders were angry because Jesus had once again broken the law by healing on the Sabbath day. Believing that law is more important than love can be a great hindrance in our ability to accept healing whenever Jesus offers it. Why were the religious authorities more concerned about Jesus' breaking the law than they were at the wonder of his healing? Didn't they want people to be healed?

We do need to cleanse our spirits before we can be made well, but sometimes we carry that idea too far. It was common in Jesus' day and still is now to think that if someone has a physical ailment, it is that person's fault. The sick person gets blamed, without compassion, because some inner evil has caused the problem. Some people proclaim that you do not get cancer unless you are angry. Or, conversely, some Christians see pain and illness as God's punishment for our sins. And if we are being justly punished, is it proper for someone to heal us?

Jesus did not think in terms of punishment but love. Healing is a great mystery. I know of one family of faith who prayed that their two-year-old would be healed of leukemia. They believed that their prayers would be answered as they desired, but the child died. Why does this child die, and that one live? We do not know. But prayer is never wasted.

If the religious leaders were offended by Jesus, there were others who wanted to make him a king, and when Jesus saw that they were coming for him, he went away to a mountain to be alone. Alone. He wanted to forgive, to love, to heal, but he had come to earth as a servant, not a king. Satan would have liked to tempt him with kingship, but that was not the calling of the incarnate One. He wanted his healing to be quiet, but people shouted it out. He told the people that he was the bread of life, but he was not understood.

No, he did not want to be king, Jesus, the bright evening Star, bringing with him wherever he went hope and joy and the promise of God's love.

★ KEEPING TRACK OF IT ALL ★

CHAPTER 9

HOW OFTEN JESUS SURPRISED AND CONFUSED HIS friends. Even his choice of disciples was surprising, and no committee today would have approved of his selection. True, fishermen were good, solid citizens, but then he went and called Matthew, a tax collector. Our tax collectors are bad enough. The rich with their clever lawyers don't pay very much, and the rest of us are bled white, but perhaps it was even worse for the Jews because they had to pay not only their local taxes, but taxes to the Romans, heavy taxes. But what did Jesus do? He picked a man who collected taxes for the Romans as one of his disciples. Not only that, but he went to have dinner in Matthew's house along with other undesirable guests—desirable people did not dine with tax collectors. The Pharisees, who were beginning to think of Jesus as a rabble-rouser, questioned his choice of dinner companions. Jesus overheard and said, "Those who are well have no need of a physician, but those who are sick. I came not to call the righteous, but sinners."

Isn't this at odds with those who insist on moral virtues as the marks of the Christian? Have we forgotten who Jesus' friends were, and who they weren't? Jesus' choice of friends did not please the Pharisees. Would Jesus choose us?

Oh, Jesus, I need you.

He was pretty clear about what he wanted. Don't fast in public. Do your good deeds quietly. And rejoice! Rejoice! While the wedding party is going on and the groom is with you, be glad. When the bridegroom is gone, then will be the time for fasting and sad faces. What are all these stories about the Bridegroom? Coming. Going. Did they know who he was? Were his stories too confusing? Was he?

Already Jesus knew that all was not well. The Good News was not being recognized. Wake up! Wake up!

But he continued his loving healing, giving sight to the blind, speech to one whose tongue was tied. And more and more often the protagonists of his stories were not the ones people might have expected; they were women and beggars and lepers and Romans and Samaritans—we don't have any equivalent today of the Samaritans, who were wholly other from "us" and even worshiped God on the wrong mountain. Was it something like the frightened fear some Protestants had of Catholics who, with their statues of saints, and the unspontaneous structure of their liturgy, could not possibly be Christians?

But Jesus' healings were there for the people to see, and they continued to question who this man might be with his compassion and his healing and his joy.

Have you ever seen the face of a surgeon who has just completed a delicate and dangerous operation and who takes off his mask to reveal eyes full of relief and joy? This gives us a glimpse of what Jesus must have looked like.

He sent his twelve closest disciples out to continue to spread the Good News, telling them not to go to the Gentiles or the Samaritans but to the lost sheep of the house of Israel. They were to take nothing with them, but depend on others for hospitality.

And already he was calling them lost sheep. Why else would he have come, except to those who had lost their way? He told the disciples the laborer is worthy of his hire, and he was fierce about those who refused to receive them. If they were not welcomed in a house they were to shake the dust of that place off their feet. Already he was beginning to be rejected. The love with which he had come from heaven to earth was beginning to be scorned and misunderstood. He warned his disciples that they, too, would be mistreated even by their families and closest friends, and that they might be brought before the courts because of him. "But don't worry about what you should say, for the Holy Spirit will teach you what you ought to say."

Hasn't it happened to us in times of crisis, words given to us that we would never have come up with ourselves? Jesus assured the disciples how much God loved them, and then again he baffled them. "For there is nothing hid except to be made manifest, nor anything secret except to come to light."

And then he further confused them by foretelling the gift of himself which he would give us in the Communion service. "I am the bread of life," he said. "Your forebears ate manna in the wilderness, and they are dead. But this is the bread which has come down from heaven, that you may eat, and not die."

What was he talking about? How could this man give his flesh to eat?

And then Jesus shocked his followers even more by saying, "Verily, verily I say unto you, except you eat the flesh of the Son of Man, and drink his blood, you have no life in you."

What!?!

Jesus was deliberately breaking the great taboo: blood. Blood is life, and blood is taboo. Women in menstrual period were unclean.

Women who were bleeding were not even fit to say prayers. Our present casualness about women's periods as simply being a normal part of the human cycle would have been incomprehensible two thousand years ago. For the women themselves the period of exile (escape?) from the family routine may have been one of the most pleasant and relaxed times of the month. They were free from all chores. They could gather together and talk about their children and their husbands and their neighbors. They could catch up on sleep. And the ritual bath after the menstrual period must have been a special joy in an arid and dusty country.

After Jesus had spoken so scandalously and mysteriously about their eating his body and blood, "from that time many of his disciples went back, and walked no more with him. Then Jesus said to the Twelve, 'Will you also go away?'"

But the twelve disciples he had chosen as his heart's companions were still faithfully with him. Nevertheless, there was continuing confusion for them. Jesus warned them of division among households, children against parents, against brothers and sisters. But no matter what, they must each take their own cross and follow him.

In the midst of miracles and stories and wonders, the shadow of the cross was falling darkly across the land.

His miracles and his love were frightening to those who looked for power, not love. The religious authorities clung to their realism and were blind to healing. It doesn't make sense but, now as then, those who want to attack are seldom held back by reason but are impelled by anger and self-righteousness.

Jesus said, "I thank you, Father, Lord of heaven and earth, that you have hidden these things from the wise and understanding and have revealed them to babies, for this was your gracious will." When children clamored around him, climbing up into his lap with their filthy little feet and hands, he forbade the disciples to take them away.

What does he mean? What is this emphasis on our being like children? How little? Little ones who confidently hold up their arms to be picked up, who climb into laps, who ask for stories, who know that it is in story that truth is found?

He said to his disciples, "Truly, whoever does not receive the kingdom of God as a little child shall not enter it." And he continued, "Whoever receives one such little child in my name receives me." And he warned them that they must never tempt a little child to sin.

I wonder who it was, and how many hundreds of years ago, who was taught to jump up on a pile of dirt or a rock and chant, "I'm the king of the castle! You're the dirty rascal!"

One of the more bewildering statements Paul ever made was, "When I was a child I thought as a child, but now I am grown up and I have put away childish things." I don't want ever to lose my child's ability to believe in the impossible. But perhaps Paul was in his middle years when he said that, those middle years when most of us feel reasonable and grown-up.

Children know how to believe the impossible, children who have not yet fallen into the game of power. Later, alas, children can be mean, deliberately hurting a weaker child. Children learn early, from their elder siblings or parents, to be unkind, to feel prejudice, to be divisive. Jesus would teach us to unlearn.

O Jesus, thank you for being born for us, God in a baby, wonderfully impossible, but true. When we stop being children and try to make this glorious love possible, we lose it.

Do we have the loving hearts of children Jesus calls us to have?

If we do not, how can we understand Jesus' love, his brightness, his laughter, his warnings, his hopes? How can we understand that what he says is true, and that the truth will make us free?

When I was a child I loved my parents, both of them. It's not very popular today to affirm that you had wonderful parents. One time at a writers' workshop I gave the assignment: "Write a story about a good mother."

There were twenty students in the class. Only one was able to write a loving story about a good mother. This evoked surprise and discussion. One writer finally said, "My mother did the best she could, with her limitations." Another said, "Was I expecting too much? Was I expecting perfection?" Another said, "It's easier to remember the things that my mother did wrong than the things she did right."

All human parents make mistakes. Mine did. I did. My children who are parents do. It is part of being human. Mostly we do the best we can with our limitations and imperfections. The most important thing we can do is to give love. Love always, no matter what. Love which truly loves enough to say no instead of the easier yes. I was sometimes angry with my kids during those inevitable times when they were terrible, but I always loved them, and I think they knew that. And I knew that my parents loved me. Therefore, I could get at least a glimpse of God's love for me and for all of creation. Jesus was always certain of the Father's love for him. There is no indication in Scripture that he ever thought of God as being angry with him. Or disappointed. Or impatient. "This," God said, "is my beloved Son in whom I am well pleased."

The Trinity: Father, Son, and Holy Spirit. Earth Maker, Pain Bearer, Life Giver. Family. We're again in a great marvel. Jesus was man and Jesus was God, and Jesus as God did not need to beg God to forgive him, since he himself was God, and neither did he need to beg God to forgive us. Forgiveness is one of the greatest gifts which Jesus gave us, his own forgiveness, and the forgiveness of the Father. It is a gift of grace, not an act of will. How often Jesus compares human love with the much greater love and forgiveness of God. How often he tries to teach us to forgive: as you forgive, so will you be forgiven. Jesus taught us with his own actions—forgiving the man who was lowered through the roof; and he taught us with his stories—the father lovingly and joyfully forgiving the prodigal son. Forgiveness is an action of love, total love.

THE FAITH OF JESUS

CHAPTER 10

IF I WANT TO HAVE THE FAITH OF JESUS, THEN IT is faith in the Father who loves him, and who loves us, who loves us so much that Jesus came to embody that love, in-carnate it.

When did the idea of an unforgiving and angry God come into the history of Christianity? Surely it is a misreading or at least a misemphasis of Scripture. God is so loving and giving that this love was expressed in Jesus.

I had never heard the phrase *substitutionary atonement* until I was in my middle years and had been invited to speak at Wheaton College. My best understanding of it is given me in Oscar Wilde's beautiful story "The Happy Prince." In the story, in the village square there is a magnificent statue of a prince encrusted with gold and jewels, with great sapphires for his eyes, and a ruby in his sword. He is covered with gold leaf and brilliant stones. Little by little, as needs arise, he gives himself away, a sapphire to a struggling student, the ruby to help a poor man buy bread for his family, his golden cloak to a freezing little girl. Little by little he gives all of himself away, his gold, his jewels, his sapphire eyes. Eventually there is nothing left of him but a lump of lead, which the village authorities see and throw on the dump heap.

This is God, completely giving away power and glory for the needs of us lost and hungry sheep. This is Jesus, faithfully fulfilling God's love in his life and death and resurrection.

With all our human struggling for power we cannot heal ourselves, so God, with wondrous love, gives away power, gives away himself so that we may be healed. We cannot do it ourselves. God does it for us.

It is again great mystery, and one which we do not express well, partly because of the change in language over the centuries. When Christopher Wren first built St. Paul's Cathedral, it was called awful, but awful wasn't what we mean by the word today. The cathedral was awe-ful in its beauty.

In Scripture we read much of the fear of God, and here again we have another word which has changed meaning in the centuries since the King James translation. According to Abraham Joshua Heschel, the word does not mean abject, cringing fear, but the awe of the glorious love of God, of the soaring beauty of St. Paul's Cathedral, or the awe that Jairus and his wife must have felt when Jesus healed their little girl, or the awe I felt as my newborn baby was given to my waiting arms.

My babies were the result of actions of love, ordinary, human love. The love of the Creator is so much greater we are blinded by the brilliance. It's too much for some of us. It threatens our power for God to give away power. We cannot bear the humility of God's love in coming to us as Jesus.

Why is there so much confusion? Have we had brutal parents? teachers who have never known love and cannot understand that it is love that made the world and all of us? A friend of mine at a church meeting was horrified when she heard a man say: "I know that I am forgiven because Jesus hung on the cross with the full weight of God's wrath and anger pouring down on him."

How could I live a life of love and joy and generosity if I thought of God as some sort of Wotan, the Norse god who threw thunderbolts?

What a sad way to live! How unhappy someone must be to forget God's love! All through both Testaments we find affirmations of God's love. God creates, looks at creation, and calls it good. God is making us with love, teaching us love by sending his own love. Jesus came to us with love, and rose from the grave for us with love, and sent us the Holy Spirit with love. Always we are surrounded by the love of the whole Trinity.

I am frightened when someone insists on a God of wrath, a God who actually hates his own creation; *his* own, yes, for surely this angry god seems to me to be masculine. Is a God of love and freedom and *Hagia Sophia* even more terrifying than a God of implacable, legalistic justice? Yes, I believe that God judges, but it is the parental judgment of love.

The love of Jesus and the faith of Jesus is shown me by my friends who have been brought up in a Christian tradition totally different from mine—and yet in our living and learning we have moved in the same direction to much the same place. All I can do is be grateful, delightedly grateful.

Thank you, God, thank you, Jesus, thank you, Holy Spirit, for loving us so much that you show your love in the extraordinary birth of Christ as a human baby, a baby who grew up to be the most exciting man to walk the earth.

He was extraordinary and he did extraordinary things. One time the disciples were in a small boat, and in the fourth watch of the night Jesus went to them, walking on the sea. And the disciples thought he was a ghost and were fearful, but Jesus said, "Be of good cheer. It is I!"

Peter said, "Lord, if it's really you [Did he doubt it?], tell me to come to you on the water."

And Jesus said, "Come."

So Peter walked on the water until he remembered that he couldn't do it, and then he began to sink, and Jesus had to pull him up.

One day on the Sabbath Jesus and his disciples were walking through the grain fields, and because they were hungry they began to pluck and eat the ears of grain. Did Jesus do this deliberately, knowing they would be seen and chastised for breaking the law on the Sabbath? Jesus calmly reminded his critics of David who ate the shewbread from the temple when he was hungry, bread which was meant only for the priests. And Jesus said to them, "The Sabbath was made for us, not we for the Sabbath." And then he said something which he must have known would infuriate them: "The Son of Man is Lord even of the Sabbath."

Not the Son of God. The Son of Man.

There it is again.

What did he mean?

Was he questioning, asking, seeing how much they understood? He tested his hearers more and more often as they understood less and less. There is a slow and subtle change as his message is not wanted by the religious leaders whose power was threatened by Jesus' own refusal of earthly power.

It is very possible for us to misinterpret Jesus' stories, refuse to understand them, but that does not mean that we should ever stop looking for truth in story, that truth which Jesus promised would set us free. What surprises us, and what we are often not willing to accept, is that Jesus' stories, and his answers to the questions put to test him, almost always turn things around, upside-down, inside out, and the tendency of the Pharisees, and our tendency today in our churches, is to try to get everything right side up again, back into the familiar boxes of recognizable laws and customs.

Jesus went from the grain fields to the synagogue, where there was a man with a withered hand, and the leaders of the synagogue asked him, "Is it lawful to heal on the Sabbath?" so that they might accuse him.

He knew they were trying to trick him, so he asked in return, "If one of your sheep falls into a pit on the Sabbath, wouldn't you pull it out? Is it lawful to do good on the Sabbath, or to do harm?" And he asked the man with the withered hand to hold it out, and he healed it. This angered the rulers of the synagogue, and they gathered together to find some wrong with which they could accuse him.

Jesus, aware of this, left, and many people followed him. He continued his loving ministry of healing, but he was mindful that those in authority were more and more suspicious of him. His parables changed, became sharper and more pointed, and some of the most difficult and even brutal ones (such as the vineyard workers killing the owner's servants, and then his son) came towards the end of his life when he was telling such stories to the very men he knew were plotting to kill him. The stories grew steadily darker as his mortal life drew to its close.

He told about the servant whose Lord forgave him his many debts, but who then went to his debtor and tried to collect the much smaller debts. And the other servants and the master were outraged at his unjust behavior.

When the seventy he had sent out returned, full of joy because of their success in healing and in driving out demons, Jesus said, "I saw Satan fall like lightning from heaven," the only time we know that he talked openly with his friends and disciples about Satan.

He continued, "Don't rejoice that the spirits are subject to you, but rejoice that your names are written in heaven."

Always the religious leaders watched him, and a lawyer tried to put him to the test by asking, "Teacher, what shall I do to inherit eternal life?"

Jesus, as he so often did, answered with a question. "What is written in the law? What do you think?"

The lawyer replied, "You shall love the Lord your God with all your heart, and with all your soul, and with all your strength, and with all your mind, and you shall love your neighbour as yourself."

Jesus said to him, "You have answered rightly. Do this and you shall live."

The lawyer, who had answered correctly, wanted to justify himself, so he asked Jesus, "And who is my neighbour?"

And Jesus told the parable of the Good Samaritan. He made it brutally clear that those who would have been expected to help the wounded man, the priest and the Levite, did not. Instead, it was a Samaritan, a Samaritan again, the last person one would have expected to be the "good guy" in the story.

He told a story about two brothers who were asked by their father to go and do some work for him. One brother said, "Of course, Father," but did not go. The other brother said, "I won't," but then went and did what the father asked.

He told them of a rich man who gathered all his riches together and planned to enjoy a life of ease and luxury. But God said, "This night your soul is required of you, and then where will all your riches be?" God is our riches. God is our treasure. Be aware always that God may come at any time. "Blessed are those servants whom the Master finds awake when he comes."

He told pointed stories of banquets to which those who had been invited did not come, and in all three synoptic Gospels he urged his followers to take up their crosses and follow him. The shadow of the cross darkened against the brilliant sunlight. The parables have become overfamiliar, so often have we heard them preached, so often have we read them, the Prodigal Son, the Foolish Virgins, Dives and Lazarus, emphasizing the hardness of the human heart versus the love of God. When Jesus heals ten lepers he asks sadly,

"Were not ten cleansed? Where are the nine? Was no one found to return and give praise to God except this foreigner?" A Samaritan, once again.

Jesus made his points plainly, often exaggerating to be certain he was understood. And when he was still not understood he was angry and surprised. His message was clear. It came directly from the Father. It was obvious. How could people not get it? How could they be so obtuse? But his anger was tempered with compassion, and tenderness for all the little ones, the outcasts, those who knew their brokenness and searched for truth. He was offended by the legalism that does not allow healing on the Sabbath; for Jesus, love was always more important than law. So, despite constant misunderstanding, he healed, he taught, he wore himself out. It is not easy for God to take on "mortal vesture," as the ancient French hymn phrases it.

Exhausted, Jesus stopped off to refresh himself at the house of his friends in Bethany, but shortly he was on the road again, preaching, telling stories, promising his listeners that God hears and answers their prayers. But then, because of the jealousy of the religious rulers, he warned them of their pride and arrogance. "Woe to you, scribes and Pharisees, hypocrites!" He was ruthless in his condemnation of pride and hardness of heart, of arrogance and legalism, and he must have known how angry this was going to make them.

Why was he such a threat to the religious rulers? They were heavy, and he was lighthearted. They fasted and he feasted with his friends. They represented the power of the religious establishment, and he represented God's vulnerability.

He continued on his way and met a young man to whom he was so drawn that he asked him to join him. But the young man, despite his immediate love of Jesus, could not give up his riches. Then came Jesus' famous remark, "It is easier for a camel to go through the eye of a needle than for a rich man to enter the kingdom of God."

They asked him, "Then who can be saved?"

Jesus looked at them and said, "With us it is impossible, but not with God. All things are possible with God."

I don't want the camel and the eye of the needle explained. The point is not that there may have been a city gate called the Needle's Eye, but that it is a marvelous metaphor, and Jesus loved metaphors.

The divine aspect of Jesus must have understood that there is no such thing as failure in God's plan. The human aspect must have been exhausted and saddened as his disciples understood less and less, his friends dwindled away, and people demanded constant signs and miracles. Even his disciples put pride of place before God's love. If they had heard his stories about taking the lowest seat at the banquet, or the last being first and the first being last, they appeared to have forgotten them.

How much worse was Judas's betrayal than the disciples' prideful pushing for power?

Judas. How are we to understand Judas? A friend of mine in Juneau, Alaska, told me that she had recently preached about Judas.

I asked her, "What did you say?"

She told me that when Judas scolded Jesus for allowing the woman to anoint his feet with expensive oil, spending money on the oil which could have been used for the poor, that was not the worst fault because we, like Judas, often fail to understand. Even when Judas contracted with the Pharisees to take money for delivering Jesus to them, that was not the worst fault, because we all do terrible things for money. Even when he betrayed Jesus by kissing him, that was still not the worst fault because one way or another we all betray our friends. But when Judas hanged himself, that was the ultimate fault, because it put a limit to the mercy of God, and we cannot do that.

But we do. We project our own limitations of mercy onto God and so, unwittingly, we join Judas in betrayal.

And why did the authorities need Judas? As Jesus pointed out, he preached daily in the temple. They could have arrested him at any time. So why did they wait, taking him deviously at night?

Even though Jesus knew that the authorities were seeking a way to condemn him to death, he continued his travels through the cities and villages, preaching the Good News of the kingdom of God. The Twelve were still faithfully with him, and a group of women, including Mary and Martha of Bethany, Joanna, Susannah, Mary of Magdala. There is nothing in Scripture to indicate that Mary of Magdala was a prostitute. She was one of the broken who came to him for healing. She had seven demons and he cleansed her of them, and then this remarkable woman became one of his followers, his friend, and one of the women who provided for Jesus and the disciples out of their own means.

He needed his friends. The tide was beginning to turn. He was even accused of casting out demons by demonic powers.

As usual, he turned away a harsh accusation with a soft answer, reminding people with his merry laugh that if Satan is divided against himself, how will his kingdom stand?

But when people want to believe evil of someone, they do not listen to reason.

One of the Pharisees asked Jesus to eat with him, a gesture of faith and friendship which Jesus accepted. A woman in the city who, according to Luke, was a sinner, came to the Pharisee's house as soon as she heard that Jesus was there. She brought an alabaster flask of fragrant oil and began to weep, and to bathe his feet with her tears, and dry them with her hair. In accepting her ministrations, Jesus was again breaking taboos. Women, good women, were not supposed to display their hair, but to cover their heads, lest the sight of their hair awaken lustful desire in men. Good Orthodox Jewish women today are still required to cover their heads. And here was this woman, obviously not a good woman, flaunting her hair as she dried Jesus' feet. In John's Gospel the woman is named as Mary of Bethany, sister of Martha and Lazarus, and this implies that this was not an ordinary, good, middle-class family. Mary not only sat at Jesus' feet to listen to him, something else women were not supposed to do, she displayed her hair. Shocking.

Today we hear a lot about the loss of family, and the need for the return of family values. As I thought about Mary and Martha and Lazarus I began to wonder what Jesus said about family and family values, and there is not a great deal in Scripture. None of the three, Mary, Martha, Lazarus, is mentioned as being married. Were they very young? There is no mention of parents.

We hear of Peter's mother-in-law, John's and Peter's parents, but little else of the family among the disciples. We hear of Jesus' brothers and sisters, but usually that they didn't understand him. We know that Jesus did not like the way women were treated. We know that Jesus and the disciples were dependent on the women who cared for them. What we think of as family is most closely represented with Jairus and his wife and daughter.

Are we limiting our thoughts? Mother, father, two or three children? Weren't Mary, Martha, and Lazarus a family? In my young to middle years I was part of what is considered a traditional family, wife, husband, three children. For a while after my husband died, my family was my two college-age granddaughters: Charlotte lived with me for seven wonderful years, and Léna was in and out. Now it is Bara, my apartment mate, who stays with me two or three nights a week. My family is my prayer group, my writers' workshops. It is my children and grandchildren and godchildren. What is family?

We are family or not largely because of the way we treat each other. We hear too much about families where there is abuse, abuse of bodies, of alcohol, of spirit. We hear of families where cheating is the highest value and the kids congregate on the street in gangs who become their families. We hear of families where things, all the things that money can buy, TVs, telephones, toys, are what matter.

I am grateful for my family, all my families.

My friend Tallis said that the Trinity is our icon of family, Father, Son, and Holy Spirit. Earth Maker, Pain Bearer, Life Giver. In a true family we honor each other. We do not control, dominate, manipulate. Power is not a family value.

Family can be a movable feast. It can be a group of friends sitting around the dining table for an evening. It can be one or two people coming to stay with me for a few nights or a few weeks. It should be the church, and I am grateful that my church is a small church. Whenever there's talk of needing a larger space, I say, sadly, that there are lots of churches in New York with large spaces. We're unique as we are. I'll be sorry if we fall into the bigger-is-better syndrome, and I'll be leaving. We have other visions for our church—helping another small but struggling church, for instance.

Family can be our house churches, our Bible study groups, our prayer groups.

Family ultimately means commitment. I am deeply committed to my family, with all its brokenness and fallenness. I am deeply committed to my friends, some of whom have been in my heart since I was a teenager, some who have come more recently. It is the commitment which makes family. The people we eat with, around the altar, or around the dining table at home.

Jesus was committed to his disciples, even when they totally failed to understand, even when they remained hung up on power, even when they abandoned him when he needed them most.

Do we sometimes run away? Do we refuse to go to the sick bed, the hospital, because it's just too hard? We're human, like the disciples.

Family forgives, as Jesus forgave.

Can we forgive the Peter or the Judas in ourselves? Jesus will. So must we.

★ I WAS BLIND, AND NOW I SEE ★

CHAPTER 11

DURING HIS HUMAN MINISTRY JESUS CONTINUED to heal, to shock, to tell stories, such as the story of the sower who sowed seed. Some of it fell on the path, and the birds came and ate it. Some fell on rock and was withered by the hot sun. Some fell on thorns, and the thorns choked it. "And some fell on good soil and brought forth grain, and yielded a great crop." And then he added, "Whoever has ears, listen," for already he was aware of how few people heard what he said, or understood what he meant, and this must have been grief to him.

He told his listeners that the parables were like lights, not to be hidden, but to be put on a stand to give light to all. And he told his friends that they were to be lights, lights not to be hidden but to give light to the world.

Jesus was light, the Light of the world, and he gave light. He opened the eyes of a man blind from birth, and again, he did this on the Sabbath day (was this deliberate?), as usual antagonizing the Pharisees, who pronounced that Jesus was a sinner because he healed on the Sabbath. This perverse legalism is still around today.

The Jewish leaders asked the man's parents, "Is this really your son, who you say was born blind? How then does he now see?"

The parents did not want to upset the religious leaders, so they told him they didn't know. "He is of age. Ask him."

And the young man said simply, "All I know is that I was blind, and now I see."

And we are left wondering, who was blind? The man blind from birth, or the Pharisees? Jesus leaves us little doubt.

It's important to remember that not all the religious leaders distrusted and hated Jesus. Joseph of Arimathea, Nicodemus, Jairus, leaders of the synagogue, all men who were important in the religious establishment, were drawn to Jesus. Their respect for him must have carried some weight, but not enough.

It is hard to understand how Jesus must have felt as he moved through the last difficult weeks, nevertheless knowing that he came from God and would return to God. Even his closeness to the Father could not take away the loneliness and seeming failure. He had to die, to be killed by those he had come to rejoice with.

So we, too, have to accept the consequences of our choices. I believe that Jesus is calling us to choose freedom with all its responsibility. It would be easier to live in a predetermined universe, where everything has already been chosen by God. Freedom is not an easy choice.

I don't think I could love a master puppeteer as I love the Holy Trinity, the Earth Maker, the Pain Bearer, the Life Giver—the Holy Spirit, the Comforter Jesus sent to be with us.

I trust that Spirit, even when the winds blow wildly. When I have a decision to make I usually ask myself what I think Jesus would do, and what Jesus would want me to do, and I do not always know the answer. I ask for the guidance of the Spirit, and I believe that it is always given, but sometimes I do not hear as I should. But I know that I am loved, even when I am not able to recognize and accept that love.

Sometimes I am given my most wondrous glimpses of Jesus in the small or unexpected things, from a friend pouring a cup of tea to looking up at the evening sky and seeing the tiny sliver of a moon and staying to watch the stars come out. I am filled with joy at the wonder of God's leaving all that glory and coming to the poor fallen thing that has become of his glorious little planet, peopled by creatures who have the ability to choose right and wrong, and who so often choose wrong. Why does this give me hope rather than despair?

I suppose it gives me hope because there is nothing that happens, nothing, that is not part of God's concern, part of that love which expressed itself completely in the Incarnation. Our wrong choices are ours, not God's. The terrible things that happen are usually because of our wrong choices.

A friend comes to tea, asking, "You mean it was not part of God's plan for Cathleen to be killed in an automobile accident?"

"No!" I exclaim. "Cathleen was killed because a drunken driver crossed the median and ran into her car. God did not make that driver drink too much." It was, once again, a human creature who had done wrong, causing pain and great anguish. God does not plan our sin and error!

"Why didn't God stop him?"

"Because God made us with free will, and that means God does not go around waving magic wands."

"But what does God do?"

"God is in it with us. That's the affirmation of the Incarnation."

"I don't like it."

"I don't, either. But I do know that I'd like a totally preplanned universe even less."

What does this kind of insistence on God's omnipotence actually do to God's loving and creative potency?

Nothing. It takes more power than I can imagine to give up power.

Perhaps this kind of thinking should change the way I pray, but it doesn't, maybe because I pray in so many different ways. I am often anxiously demanding. Fix it. Do something. Save. Help.

God isn't just sitting back watching the universe unfold. God does not interfere with free will, and yet God is the Creator of the great dance of being, participating, loving. Sometimes the paradox makes sense to me only as I hold out my hands for the bread and wine.

Do I believe in miracles, then? Of course I do. I have seen miracles, participated in miracles, and I don't want them explained away. Nor do I try to reconcile these miracles with God's precious gift of free will.

Jesus said, "Anything you ask in my Name I will give you."

A family in my church prayed faithfully and with complete trust as they watched their daughter die of cancer, a young woman who was a physician working among the poorest of the poor, who had given her life to good. What did Jesus mean? Not that he would always answer yes, but what did he mean? When he gave that promise, what did he mean?

We had no answer.

Does it have something to do with eternity, rather than time? Is it that their daughter was a holy person and reconciled to her death, and ready for it, but they were not? Jesus does not break promises, but we may not yet be able to understand the way he keeps them.

Cathleen. A two-year-old baby with leukemia. A brilliant young doctor. It is beyond our comprehension. We want to understand, and it is difficult to accept that we cannot, because we used to be able to say, "It is God's will." But healing is God's will. If we could understand everything we would have absolute power, and that is not what Jesus came to give us.

God gives each of us our own way to be part of the suffering of the world, and part of the joy of the world, too.

One morning in church I watched a couple whose dearly wanted baby was colicky and wailed constantly so that there was no sleep to be had for child or parents, and all three looked white and drawn and exhausted and yet the mother and father had nothing but joy in their eyes as they tried to hush their screaming infant before taking her out so she could cry without disturbing the service.

And then I wondered about the Rwandan babies and the Bosnian babies and the Abyssinian babies whose little stomachs were not going to be filled and who were not going to stop crying. And I knew they were why Christ left the star-flung heavens and came to us to be part of all the pain and suffering. And the joy. And I remembered that the first recorded miracle in the Bible was at a wedding, two people coming together in love, that marvelous love which is never completely understood. And I knew that we do not have to understand, we do not have to understand anything except that the Maker loves us enough to come and be part of us.

That is what matters.

When we try to explain it, we lose it. When we try to explain the stories which have grown up around God's love we lose the love in the midst of the explanations, because love defies explanations. What matters is not whether Adam and Eve were actual, provable, existing people or whether they had belly buttons, but that God in infinite love peopled this lovely little planet for us to care for and expected that we would love each other, and that we would therefore love the God who made it all.

As long as our explanations are stories, seeking after truth rather than fact, we need not fear them. But when they become finite answers to infinite questions they contribute less to knowledge than to divisions and hatred and tears in heaven.

Unless an answer is "I love you," it is apt to cause pain, not explanation.

O, God, I love you, for you love me, and love begets love.

As I contemplate the love of God which has sustained me for nearly eighty years, and still sustains, I think of Jesus' young life being cut off, Jesus' being misunderstood, hated by some, loved by a few who, despite Peter's declaration that Jesus was the Christ, still did not understand. When Jesus tried to explain to his disciples the difficulties ahead, Peter cried out, "God forbid! This shall never happen to you."

Jesus' next words were, "Get behind me, Satan, for you are not on the side of God, but of man."

These were hard words, and the disciples did not want to hear them. In effect, they closed their ears and refused to hear.

Six days went by and Jesus took Peter and James and John with him and went up to a high mountain, "and he was transfigured before them, and his face shone like the sun and his garments became white as light."

And Moses and Elijah appeared, talking with him.

And bumbling Peter wanted to build three booths, to keep them there. Back in their safe little boxes. Back right side up again.

The Transfiguration was, indeed, incomprehensible, and the disciples did not comprehend.

And a voice came out of the cloud saying, "This is my beloved Son. Hear him."

Listen! Listen!

And suddenly the three disciples were alone with Jesus.

It was a moment of glory which preceded the darkness of the days which were to follow. How often people want mountaintop experiences, more, please, more! But Jesus' disciples had only that one. The rest of the time they slogged along the dirty roads in the glaring heat, not knowing what was going to happen next.

Not knowing.

Peter, James, and John did not know what Jesus was showing them in that blinding light of the Transfiguration. Was it ordinary light? Or was it the light which Christ originally knew, uncreated light? They did not know whether they had dreamed, or whether they had actually seen what they had seen. As far as we know, after Peter's suggestion of three tabernacles, they did not speak of it. Mortal language, human understanding, was not adequate.

A few days later Jesus tried again to alert them. He knew that he had antagonized the religious leaders beyond any hope of reconciliation. Perhaps Moses and Elijah had warned him of that, and affirmed his willingness to stay human, the mortal man who had to be with his brothers and sisters as they were, not as a god who could play at being mortal and who, when things got tough, would leave them to be God again. Jesus kept his promise to be human for us so that we might be human, too. It is difficult for us to understand his dual nature, but impossible if we diminish his humanity. Our understanding will not come in ordinary, mathematical proofs or equations, but in flashes of the reality of love, a reality which is often most honestly faced in the world of dream, myth, parable, and questions which have no finite answer.

Jesus knew that when he returned to Jerusalem, he would be going to his death, and he knew that this death would probably be by crucifixion because that was the worst punishment that the Romans allowed the Jews to give.

The cross. Oh, what about the cross! Everything in me rebels at the idea that the cross was part of God's plan. The cross may have been inevitable, just as Cathleen's death was inevitable when the drunken driver hit her car, but it was not preplanned. God knew that Jesus' actions would lead to the cross, that his Son would die, but his love was so great that he would not interfere.

In my ears I hear a sort of midrash, the feminine in the Trinity exclaiming, "You planned what? Your own son? Are you crazy? That's a terrible plan. No loving father would plan to crucify his own son. What are you thinking of? You almost made this mistake once before, and I had a terrible time finding a ram in time. But this—No. This is not a plan. This is not possible. This is not love."

"Should I stop it?"

"Of course not. You know power is not what it is about. But you don't plan it."

No. Love is what it is about. Love is God.

If God is God, how much does God know? Is there anything that God does not know? The Russian theologian Nicholas Berdyaev believed that there were times when God chose not to know, in order not to deprive us of any of our freedom. But I think it's more complex than that, and more difficult for us to understand. We human creatures live and know in time, whereas God also knows in eternity, which is not limited by time. Eternity is not a time concept. So the powerful paradox I live with is that God could know about the cross without planning it. In God's eyes, the story is complete in eternity. To our limited way of thinking, God knows yesterday, today, tomorrow.

As Jesus points out, only God knows the moment of the Second Coming, and God is not telling, not even Jesus, not even the holy angels in heaven. God's way of knowing the entire story is something we time-bound creatures can't even begin to comprehend. Occasionally the saints and mystics are given glimpses, but they are only glimpses.

This does not mean a blank nothingness in our comprehension. In my childhood my father could not promise me that there would never be another war because he could see the lineup of the nations and where the tensions and angers were leading. My mother did not have to be a doctor (or God) to know that my father was dying. I did not have to have any special knowledge to know that when we left Europe and returned to the U.S.A. and to the South, not home to New York, things were going to be different.

There are terrible questions to be asked as we think about the nature of love and the nature of God.

A young woman comes to tea, bringing her three-month-old baby and her deepest questions. "Madeleine—"

"Yes?"

She brushes her lips gently over the baby's soft, sparse hair, then raises her eyes to mine. "God is love? You believe that?"

I know what is coming. I answer softly, "Yes."

"Then what about the cross?"

"God did not stop it."

"Could it have been stopped?"

"If God is God, yes."

"But—what my Sunday school teacher said—the cross was something God already knew about before Jesus was born. God arranged it." She shudders, holding her baby close. "I wouldn't. I would never plan to kill my baby. On purpose. I don't know what's going to happen tomorrow, or ten years from now. I know I can't stop my baby from being hurt . . . but I'd never plan it ahead of time."

Oh, God. Fumblingly I try to tell her my thoughts about time and eternity.

Do we dare allow God the free will that God gave us?

But she asks, "Does a God of love preplan the terrible death of a beloved Son in a hideous, painful way before that Son is even born? Was it really the way a loving Father would deliberately choose before he sent his only begotten Son to us for love of us?"

No. No. That is not how it is.

Dear God, how could you give us free will if you have no free will yourself? Does God's free will conflict with God's complete vision in eternity?

The young mother bounces her baby, and the little one crows with pleasure. "Babies used to die of diphtheria, but God didn't plan for them to have diphtheria?"

"No," I say.

"And then there was polio and now there are other weird new diseases, and that insurance company sent a baby home from the hospital too soon and the baby died, but God didn't plan all this. I could never plan anything that would hurt my child just to make some kind of point."

"No," I agree.

"But when my baby had a cold last week I did everything I could to help. I sat up all night and rocked and sang and loved."

"And loved," I say.

"And when the baby cried, I cried, too."

"You know the story of Noah and the flood?" I ask.

She looks startled. "Yes."

"There's a story that God was so sad at what was happening to his people that he wept for forty days and forty nights. God's tears made the flood."

Someone suggested, "Did [God] plan it? If I sent my child into a
street, knowing that the child will never survive that street alive, did
I plan her death? I think so. Even though I am not the one running
her over, I knew it would happen and I intended it because I sent
her there. In that sense, to me, God planned the Crucifixion."

This is, to me, a horrible, unthinkable example. What mother
would deliberately send her child into the street, knowing that the
child will be killed? Wouldn't the mother hold the little girl's hand?
I don't believe that the writer of this example would ever do what
she suggests. She continues, "But [the Crucifixion] was not pre-
meditated murder."

Wasn't it? Isn't it murder to send your child into the street
knowing that she is going to be killed?

We flawed, limited human beings do not know what God knows.
We only know, from reading and rereading Scripture, that God
loves. That is enough. Do not try to explain it to me, and I will not
try to explain it to you.

Let all mortal flesh keep silence,
And with fear and trembling stand,
Ponder nothing earthly minded,
For with blessing in his hand
Christ our God to earth descendeth,
Our full homage to demand.

King of Kings, yet born of Mary,
As of old on earth he stood,
Lord of lords in human vesture,
In the body and the blood

He will give to all the faithful
His own self for heavenly food.

It is the mystery of love. That is enough.

★ MY BRIGHT EVENING STAR ★

CHAPTER 12

GOD'S LOVE DOES NOT LESSEN THE IMPACT OF Jesus' dying on the cross but enlarges it. God has come to us and even gone to death for us, because love will not tamper with the free will given us, even though that free will leads to our death, our death far more than Jesus' death. But God loves us so much that Jesus' death is used to kill death. Adam couldn't make it, didn't love God enough to obey. But Jesus did, loved God enough so that he was willing, in his humanness, to go to a death that his divinity could have prevented.

He had raised people from the dead, the son of the widow of Nain, Jairus's daughter, Lazarus—Lazarus who had been dead for four days.

Jesus called Lazarus from the grave and set off for Jerusalem.

Again he warned his disciples, telling them that he would be mocked and shamefully treated and spat upon, and that he would be scourged and killed, and on the third day he would rise.

But they understood none of these things. Instead, James and John asked that they might sit, one at his right hand, one at his left in his glory.

Had they heard nothing?

And again he told them that he had come to them not as a king but as one who serves.

When they drew near to Jerusalem and came to the Mount of Olives, Jesus sent two of his disciples: "Go into the village opposite you, and immediately as you enter it you will find a colt tied, on which no one has ever sat; untie it and bring it. If anyone says to you, 'Why are you doing this?' Say, 'The Lord has need of it.'"

A crowd followed, and people threw down their garments and palm branches. "Blessed is he who comes in the name of the Lord."

"Hosannah in the highest!"

It was a raggle-taggle procession. Many had already left him. He entered Jerusalem, and taught, and told stories. He told of a man who planted a vineyard and let it out to tenants. When the time came, he sent one of his servants to collect his dues, but the tenants beat him and sent him away empty-handed. Then he sent other servants, and they were equally evilly treated. Finally he sent his son, saying,

154

"They will respect my son." But the wicked tenants killed the son.

When the chief priests and the Pharisees heard his parables, they could not help knowing that Jesus was speaking about them. His last parables were told to the very people who were going to kill him. He would not have told this story at the beginning of his mission. Now, as he neared his death, the stories changed.

He stood over Jerusalem and mourned, "Oh, Jerusalem! Jerusalem!"

He warned his friends of the terrible troubles that were to come and urged them to be ready, "for the Son of Man is coming at an hour you do not expect."

Was he aware, then, that Judas was going to the chief priests in order to betray him? Did he know why? Did Judas know why? We can make guesses, that Judas perhaps was trying to force his hand, to get him to forget that he had promised to come to us mortals as one of us, and throw out a divine thunderbolt or two, but we will never know.

Meanwhile they prepared for the Passover. As they gathered together he warned them that one of them sitting at table with him was going to betray him. And they began to question one another, and perhaps not one of them was entirely sure of his own loyalty.

As they were eating, Jesus took bread and blessed it and said, "This is my body." And then he took the wine and said, "Drink you all of this," and so began the holy mysteries we know when we, too, meet together, for bread, and for wine.

It is indeed a holy mystery, and when we try to define it we lose it, as we lose the truth of story when we confuse truth and fact.

Even at the Last Supper once again his disciples began to argue about which of them was to be regarded as the greatest. It is hard to believe. But would we have been any less selfish? And, yet again, Jesus reminded them that he had come as a servant, not as a lord.

Had Jesus expected that his message of Good News would be received with joy? That his chosen disciples would understand him and stay with him in his time of need? That Judas would be trustworthy, not only with caring for the money of the disciples, but in his faith in Jesus? Did Jesus know the potential for denial in Peter when he called him from the fishnets?

Shouldn't God have suggested fewer healings on the Sabbath? Couldn't he have urged Jesus to be more tactful?

Not if Christ came to us as Jesus, fully human. And isn't that what the Incarnation is all about?

They sat at the table together for that last meal, and he warned Peter that he was going to deny him. The other disciples were too busy arguing about who was going to be greatest to give any thought to the suffering of their Master. It took no prescience on Jesus' part, no calling on the divine aspect of himself, to know what lay ahead.

Peter cried out, "Lord, I am ready to go with you to prison and to death."

Jesus said, "I tell you, Peter, that the cock will not crow this day until three times you deny that you know me."

He went to the garden to pray, taking Peter, James, and John with him, and even then, seeing their Master's visible anguish, they could not keep their hearts alert with him but fell into sleep. They were the three disciples with whom Jesus was most intimate, who went with him to the Mount of Transfiguration, but they, even they did not have the strength to wait with him.

So Jesus had to struggle alone. Perhaps this was Satan's final temptation. Did he insinuate, "You don't have to go through with this, you know. Crucifixion is a horrible death. You're God as well as mortal, Jesus. Isn't it about time you forgot the mortal part and used your divinity to get out of this horror? You've failed in your mission. Nobody understands you. Nobody knows what you're all about, so why not say—if you'll pardon me—to hell with it and just go back to heaven? Or, if you insist on trying to help these idiots, let them crucify you and then leap down from the cross. That would be more spectacular than turning stones into bread."

And Jesus turned from Satan and turned to God, praying with drops of sweat like blood. "Oh, God, if you're willing, take this cup from me. Nevertheless not my will, but yours, be done." To the religious leaders he was a blasphemer and a criminal and according to their law he deserved crucifixion.

He was not asking if God wanted him to be crucified. He was asking, "Do I have to do it? Stay human till the very end? Die like a mortal? a criminal? I know that I have not been understood, except by a few, and that people want power, not love. Do I have to keep on offering love, as a mortal, not as God, but as one of these strange creatures I came to join? If I die, will they understand? Or will it all have been for nothing?"

And Satan came in again, saying, "Nothing. You're absolutely right. It has all been for nothing. Look. Let me show you just a few little things that are going to happen in the next few thousand years, and all because of you. Start with just a short while after your death, and look at all those people out on the street killing each other, with rage and hatred on their faces. Do you know why? They're fighting about the Arian heresy, about whether there was a time when the Son was not. Funny, when you think about it, isn't it? And then there was the Albigensian heresy, and that will cause lots of bloodshed, too. Now let's jump to the split between the Christians of the East and West, and don't forget the Crusades. Or the men of science who were burned at the stake because they opened up the universe, your universe, I might add. And then of course there are the Protestants and the Catholics and the literalists and the—"

No. No.

"Oh, yes." Satan smirked and smeared the air with the most terrible of temptations. "How much more harm has been done in your name, Jesus, than good? Change it now, Jesus. Flame into God with your power and change it."

And Jesus turned from Satan with drops of sweat like blood.

And what did God want?

What was the Father's will?

Was it not love?

Satan was clever. Jesus could have avoided the cross, but he did not. He took with him onto the cross all the sins that had ever been committed since Adam and Eve disobeyed God. He took those sins on him when he was born, but then he took them as a baby, and now he took them as a grown man, knowing what they really were, how terrible, how death-dealing. But also knowing that Satan was (and is) the father of lies. And Jesus was and is the Son of Love. Satan is the great deceiver, tempting us with half-truths. Satan grasped after power. Christ opened his hands and let power go, falling through his fingers like so much sand.

Knowing the horror that lay ahead, Jesus rose from prayer and Judas came and kissed him, the prearranged signal.

Jesus was seized and led to Caiaphas, and all his disciples fled from him in terror, all of them, abandoned him to be accused and condemned and screamed against.

Peter at least hung around the courtyard where Jesus had been taken, but three times vehemently denied that he had had anything to do with him. "I do not know the man of whom you speak." And immediately the cock crowed, and Jesus turned and looked at him, and Peter went out and wept bitterly.

Peter wept. Judas killed himself. The other disciples hid. Pilate tried to save Jesus, but could not, for the rage of the crowd screamed "Crucify him! Crucify him!"

Barabbas was spared instead of Jesus, Barabbas who had led an insurrection against Rome, and who had murdered, Barabbas, whose name means "Son of the Father," whereas Jesus called himself the "Son of Man."

Jesus was led out to be crucified, carrying the great crossbar of the crucifix, because the uprights were permanently set in the ground. He was exhausted, his feet stumbling. When they saw a man of Cyrene, Simon by name, they gave him the cross to carry. And that is somehow a comfort and a lesson. Jesus did not carry his own cross the whole way. Simon carried it for him. So we, too, may accept help when the cross is too heavy. And sometimes we are called to be Simon and carry the cross for someone else.

Jesus was nailed to the cross and the disciples were not there in his agony, except for John, who stood with Mary, his mother, and Mary Magdalene and Martha and Mary and some of the other women, and the sword must have pierced all the way through his mother's heart.

The crowd shouted and mocked. "If you're the Christ, come down from the cross, come down, that we may see and believe."

And he could have, and Satan knew that he could have. Was that what Judas had hoped for? But Jesus, Son of Man, stayed there, keeping his promise.

And there was thunder and the veil of the temple was rent and God shook the earth. God was not silent. God was there.

Jesus was taken down from the cross and his dead body was laid in his mother's arms. Joseph of Arimathea, who was a respected member of the council but who also loved Jesus, offered his own tomb, and Jesus was wrapped in a clean shroud and taken there, and then a stone was rolled against the door of the tomb.

When Mary of Magdala went to the sepulcher, that stone had been rolled away and she was frantic. She asked a man she thought was a gardener if he knew where they had taken her Lord. And Jesus called her by name, and she knew him. It was Jesus! Imagine the joy of that moment of recognition! It was all love affirmed in a moment of glory.

When the other women came the angel told them that Jesus was risen, and they went with great joy and told the disciples what had happened, but they were not believed. (Why are women often not believed?) But at last Peter and John came to the tomb, and then Jesus spoke to the couple on the road to Emmaus.

We know that one of the two was Cleopas, but the other is not named, so perhaps she was Cleopas's wife.

Finally Jesus appeared to the disciples and ate fish with them, and at last they believed the impossible, the wondrous, glorious impossible marvel of the Resurrection.

When Jesus asked Peter three times if he loved him, did Peter realize that Jesus was redeeming the three times Peter rejected him? Did Jesus' friends understand the amazing change that had happened within them? Turning them from defeated shadows to radiant lovers?

Oh, thank you, Jesus, for being born for us, and living for us, and dying for us, and rising for us, and sending us the Holy Spirit. Thank you, with thanks that are beyond words, but must be expressed in the lovingness of our lives.

Love. Love is not power, but is that humility which leads to freedom. A terrifying freedom!

161

Do we want freedom? Dostoevsky's Grand Inquisitor was certain that we did not, and that Jesus has done us great harm in offering it.

We want security. We want comfort. We want affluence. None of these give us freedom. But there is no such thing as certain security. We never know what is going to happen, what news we'll be given when the phone rings, what horror story will break into the television program we're watching. I have children and grandchildren, and they give me vulnerability, not security. In my immediate family in the past year we've had the terror of life-threatening diseases, automobile accidents, broken marriages. It has been a year of anxiety and grief—and love. And joy, the joy of weddings, birthdays, puppies, parties. And love. Love offers us the greatest joy and the greatest pain.

We all want comfort. How many television commercials offer us pills against any kind of pain? We've become a pill-popping nation, and it is important to relieve pain, to take medication for problems which can and need to be corrected. But it is not helpful to take pills for the slightest ache. Our bodies have their own defenses against pain, and when we keep turning to popular chemicals, we lower those defenses.

We're thought of as an affluent country, though right now the rich are getting richer and the poor are getting poorer. I want enough money for shelter, a healthy diet, a comfortable mattress, enough clothes to keep me warm in winter. Affluence has not helped us as a nation; it has softened us. When we are soft we are less free. When we are less free we are less human.

Beyond the split between the flabby permissivists and the rigid fundamentalists are the sects and cults which are proliferating. In the sects and cults freedom is relinquished for answers, answers to everything. Every question has to have an answer. There are rules to follow, and they can be followed without thinking because they promise that you and your group are going to be saved. It has become all right to dislike, distrust, and even hate other groups, because your group is the chosen one. Keep your guns; it is your right. Hate your neighbour; he doesn't think the way you do. Tell people what they can read and what they cannot read. Give them your list of those you think are candidates for heaven, and consign the others to hell. And you will have power.

And it doesn't work. It never has worked.

When we read the Gospels, and, indeed, Scripture in general, we see the same message, over and over again. Love. As I grow older and love more and more people I am more and more vulnerable. My husband died and I miss him daily. We had forty years of marriage and I am grateful, but his death is still grief to me and will always be so. And I would not want it otherwise. The freedom Jesus offers me contains within its vastness the freedom to grieve, not to become addicted to grief, but to learn to live with it.

I don't always want freedom. I want security. I want comfort. I want nothing to go wrong, nobody I love to be hurt, to disappoint me. But that is not what Jesus offered. He offered life, and life more abundantly, and that means everything, the whole spectrum, laughter and tears, joy and disappointment, but above all life lived fully and openly and appreciatively. That is how Jesus lived, and how we are to live.

There is much to weep for, and much to be thankful for. Little things. Big things. Little ones blowing soap bubbles. Cooking in pots that came to me from my grandmother. Serving from a dish bought in Iona. Thanking the street woman who helped me across a snowdrift. Being grateful for enough covers on my bed at night, for clean sheets and pillowcases. For a hot, soaky bath. Being grateful, ultimately, that I have been given strength to get through a lot of major and minor vicissitudes of life and that I am stronger because of them. Hoping that the freedom that Jesus offers me is going to give me strength and courage and humor to get through whatever comes.

Freedom is a frightening gift, but it was what Jesus gave us, the freedom to forget power and become human. Our addiction to power is nothing new. It goes all the way back to Adam and Eve.

Jesus' human actions had human consequences. He was steeped in Hebrew Scripture, in the prophets, but his response was a human response along with his quiet acceptance of the divine. As a young man he was full of the joy of his message, and he did not, I believe, expect it to be rebuffed and rejected by the religious leaders. The terrible loneliness of his last weeks was something he had to go through. Even his closeness to the Father could not take the anguish of those last weeks away. He had to die, to be killed by those with whom he had come to rejoice.

But he could not be killed. Power could be killed, but not humility.

And then the sun rose and Jesus was alive and terror fled and the Resurrection was an inner brightness as glorious as the outer brightness of the Transfiguration. And that light, inner and outer, began its journey around the earth, the solar systems, the furthest galaxies, light that is not power, but is wholly love.

O Jesus, my Companion, my Guide upon the way, morning star to evening star—what wondrous love is this! God so loved the world that the Creator of it all came to be with us.

Then, and now, and forever.

Thank you. Amen. Alleluia.

Crosswicks Cottage
1 January 1997